Global Travels of God's Servants

By Connie Smith

Third Edition

By Connie Smith

© 2011 by Connie Smith

ISBN: 978-1-329-62981-3

Table of Contents

Chapter	Page

Chapter   Page

Dedication

This book is lovingly dedicated to our daughter Penny Smith, who has been encouraging me for a long time to write it down. For her, here it is!

Note to the Reader

The original manuscript of this book was titled *"Our Adventures in Europe,"* because those adventures contained the most exciting stories. Our first European adventures were in 1980, and our second European adventures were in 1982. We completed the manuscript on October 22, 2009. Six years later, on October 18, 2015, we decided to edit the manuscript and change the title to *"Global Travels of God's Servants."* We changed the title because we now feel that our trips to the Philippines, our travels throughout the United States and Canada, and the trip to Haiti are just as important as the trips to Europe.

The next portion of our lives is another book. If God so leads, I will write it; if he doesn't, I won't. He is, always has been, and always will be the boss. Here we are now: It is many years later, and we are much older and we feel much wiser. We would go again if we heard God's voice saying to do just that. At this time of our lives, we feel the ministry shifting again: Now, people come to *us* instead of us going to *them*. It is the will of our Father.

We are peaceful, fulfilled, happy, and content; and we are rich in experiences and in God's ways. We have a greater love for God *now* than we had back *then*. We have a small Bible Study in our home, and we are connected with others around the country who love us; and they come periodically to speak and share. We have wonderful, powerful, Spirit-anointed gatherings right here in our humble home. We are in the center of God's very perfect will. What, may I ask, is any better than that?

We are not looking to escape into some Rapture or into some heaven. Our heaven is in our hearts. Jesus said that, "...the kingdom of God is within you." (Luke 17:21) We don't need to look for it anywhere else. Dean and I walk and live in God's presence every day, and that is joy unspeakable and full of glory.

Our prayer for this book is that, by reading it, your life will be challenged: Your eyes will be enlightened, your ears will be opened, and our great heavenly Father will become *real* to you. If we, two common, ordinary, Michigan farmers could hear and obey God's will, so can *you*! There is nothing too hard for our God. Believe and obey! It will carry you around the world. It is better than any theological education.

Obedience is better than sacrifice, and to hearken than the fat of rams. (1 Sam. 15:22)

The Kingdom of God is not meat nor drink, but righteousness, and peace, and joy in the Holy Ghost. (Romans 14:17)

Introduction

This is a story about two very ordinary people that met the Lord Jesus at an early age. We both loved him as much as we were taught to, and as much as we knew how too. In 1971, we received the baptism of the Spirit, and from then on, our lives changed dramatically. It is from that experience that the life-changing events, recorded in this book, took place. Our prayer is that you will be blessed and be thrilled with what the Lord did for us; and *through* us, be challenged in your own lives to always answer the call of the Spirit.

Chapter 1: Early Years

1a: In the Beginning

Let me begin by saying that my husband Dean and I are two average people with a high school education. We both grew up on farms about 2 miles apart in Port Huron, Michigan. We came from parents that seemed to struggle financially most of their lives. They worked very hard, but they never were able to accumulate much of this world's goods. When we were growing up, neither Dean nor I realized that, in this world's eye, our families would have been considered poor. However, we never *felt* poor: We had clothes to wear and a clean house to live in, and we never went hungry. When you don't know any different, you are not aware that there are others living in much better conditions. Neither set of parents fought, and we felt loved; and really, that is all that is important.

We both grew up with a great deal of responsibility, and we had many chores as children growing up, but we never argued about it. It was the way it was, and we did not question it as many do today. Because of the responsibility that we were used to, we really matured early. Dean came from a family of four children, and I came from a family of two, just my brother and I. My mother worked at a small grocery store, so there was a great deal of cleaning chores that I assumed at a young age. Dean's mom was a stay-at-home mother, but with so many in the family and no running water, there was a lot of hard work involved.

With our both coming from farms, we were used to all the work that that entails. We were up early every day, and we had to feed the pigs, chickens, cows, horses, geese, dogs, cats, goats, ducks, etc. Then, we had to clean, milk, water, brush, etc. Along with the daily tasks, there were the crops to plant as well, for we had a large garden for canning. We also had the summer job of taking in the hay. Everything we did, we did the old-fashioned way, so that meant longer times involved and much more handwork. We slept well at night, for we were really exhausted. There was no energy to get into mischief back then. We learned at an early age what endurance was all about, and it was to serve us well when we were called later by the Spirit to make our journeys into Europe.

Dean and I were both post-depression babies. Dean was born in June of 1934, and I came along in

July of 1937. The world was still trying to get up and moving again economically when we made our appearance. Both of us had almost the same background as far as our being conservative of all things, both in the natural and man-made: Our families lived from the earth and the animals we kept. When I look back now, I realize that we really had a good life, meaning that we ate all organic foods and knew what it was to work hard and feel a sense of accomplishment in all we did.

Dean and his siblings picked blueberries every summer to help pay for their school clothes. Every day, during the berry season, they were in the patch picking early in the morning. They had their regular customers every year, so they were able to sell all they picked. If you have never picked wild blueberries, you have no idea as to the mosquitoes, the scratches from the bushes, and the work involved to gather even *one* quart. We learned that, when we picked, we didn't eat, or we didn't make the money. In our lives, we could not quit until the job was done. I remember very well: We grew raspberries, and I really disliked picking *any* kind of berries, but my lot was to pick them. Our farm sat on a hill, and I could watch the other young people in the area go past our house on the way to the old swimming hole in Pine River. When I would be in the raspberry patch, oh how I would hate my job even more. The sun would beat down, and the sweat would run down my face. The bushes had thorns, and I would end up all scratched up. As a young girl of about 13 or 14, I wanted, in the worst way, to be on my horse and heading for the river also. I was taught that you did not quit until the job was finished, and at times, the rows of raspberry bushes looked *endless*. We were

5

taught perseverance at young ages, and that also served us well in our work behind the Iron Curtain.

1b: Young Love

Dean and I met quite young. We lived 2 miles apart, and as I said before, in the country, that is not considered far. Dean and my brother Ron had been in some classes together in school, so they were well acquainted. Dean was involved with a Baptist Church in his youth, and I was in the same kind of Church but in a different part of the city. Every month, the Churches would have a skate night at a roller skating rink nearby. I would attend as well as Dean, but never together. I would watch him on those nights from afar, as he would skate with all the older girls: After all, I was 3 years younger than he was. I knew in my young heart, even then, that I was so in love with him, and he didn't know I even *existed*. You know how we young girls think: I felt that I would surely *die* if he wouldn't notice me. Every time these nights would occur, I would spend most of the time looking and longing, and I would go home *frustrated*, because he acted like I wasn't even there.

This continued for quite some time, possibly about 1 year. I finally said to my brother, "Please tell that man to take me out on a date." Of course, you know how brothers are, and for a long time, nothing was done or said. I finally begged him to tell Dean to take me out so often that he complied just to get me off his back.

One Sunday afternoon, we heard a knock on the door: I answered it, and it was *Dean*. I almost fainted from shock. He came in and just talked to all of us, my parents and me, for the entire afternoon. My parents loved him right away, and I was already in love with him. Actually, I *had* been in love with him for some time, so I was in *heaven* having him there. My heart was doing flips the entire time. When I walked him to the door, he asked me to go with him the following night to a concert in Sarnia, Canada. Sarnia is one mile from Port Huron, Michigan, and it is just across the Blue Water Bridge. I said "Yes" so fast that I probably looked over-anxious, but I didn't care, for my dreams were finally coming true.

I could hardly wait for the next night to come. I was so nervous, excited, and happy. He came to pick me up right on time, and we went to Canada for the concert. My heart beat so fast during the whole evening that I could hardly stand it. I was filled with joy that my dreams of so long were finally coming to pass. We went out to a small hamburger place afterward, and then we just talked and talked and talked. I knew right away that I was a goner, and he was the only one for me. From that night on, we never dated anyone else nor even *wanted* to. Our love was young, strong, and so wonderful!

We dated for 5 months, and then Dean gave me a ring and asked me to marry him. I was 16 and he was 19 at the time. We began dating in April of 1953, and we married in January 23 of 1954. It was only a nine-month courtship, and my father struggled with my marrying so young. My mother's wisdom won out: She knew that Dean was good for me, and he was a good man all around. So my dad consented. Dean had a good job with Western Electric, which is (or *was*) the installation-and-manufacturing division for Bell Telephone Company at that time. He was in the apprentice program for his job, so the pay was small, but regular.

Our wedding was in the South Park Baptist Church, and we were married by my minister

Thomas Harfst. The Church was full, and we received many gifts. It was a cake, punch, and coffee affair. With our being so young and so passionately in love, the wedding seemed to last forever, for all we wanted was to get away from all of them. We went north for our honeymoon, and we spent about three days just traveling around and getting used to each other. We returned to my mother and father's farm afterward.

1c: Our First Home

We purchased an 18-foot trailer that someone had been using for camping or hunting. There was no bathroom in it, and in those days, when you rented space in a park, there were usually bathrooms and laundry facilities located on the grounds. My husband's job was such that he traveled with his work, so our first home was in Flint, Michigan. We pulled our little home there and set it up. We had completely gone through it: We had painted and varnished all the way through. It was a very attractive little home to begin our married life in. We were so much in love, so we didn't notice all the inconveniences.

We became active in a small Baptist Church nearby and settled into married life quite easily. I had trouble with being lonely for home, and I do think that it had to do with my being so young. Dean would get lonely for his home as well, and so we would spend many weekends with the parents. We would leave on Friday night after Dean's workweek was over, and we would stay until Sunday night when we would return home in the dark. We would make the weekend last as long as possible.

Our little trailer home did not have a refrigerator; it only had an icebox. So, many times, on Sunday nights, we would have to stop and pick up a block of ice for 50 cents to keep our food cold. It was a simple life for us, and I tried to do some odd jobs to help out in the trailer park. I got acquainted with a bachelor there, and he let me do his laundry and wash his windows for a few dollars. It helped out a lot, because Dean was making $48.00 per week take-home pay, and we owed $35.00 on the trailer and $35.00 on lot rent each month. I do believe that we were paying on the car as well, and so there was very little left over each week.

Back then, we paid 25 cents per gallon for gas, so we would put a dollar's worth in the tank, take our two-man pup tent, and go *camping* lots of weekends. We had a Coleman gas stove and a cooler, and we would take some hotdogs and have a really good time, for we were used to the *simple* things of life. Dean really loved *fishing* in those early years, and so we would fish, and fish; and at the end of the weekend, we would head back to our little trailer home. That seemed to be our pattern of life in those early days of marriage.

After about 6 months of this, our car broke down. We didn't have the money for lot rent and fixing the motor of the car, so we pulled the little trailer to my parents' farmyard and had the car engine overhauled. We paid payments on the repairs until it was paid off, and we stayed in my parents' backyard. We went into the house to bathe, wash clothes, and use the toilet facilities; but otherwise, we were in our little home. Dean would get up very early and drive to his job. It was about an hour-and-a-half away from my parents, and he would be very tired from the drive each day, but he did what was necessary for us to survive.

1d: The Job Moves North

I think it was another two or three months when Dean got transferred to Clare, Michigan. It was so wonderful, as he received *transfer* pay for his time there. It gave us about $50.00 more each week, and we really felt *rich*. I remember going to the grocery store after Dean received his first check that was larger: I was able to buy some *spices* that I had wanted for a long time, and it felt so *wonderful* to be able to do that.

We were in a little trailer park, and the same situation was available to us as in Flint. We had to go to the park facilities to shower, wash clothes, and use the bathroom. It was winter, and I was inside all the time. It was a small space to be confined to, and after a while, I developed a spastic colon. I had a series of tests, and the conclusion was that I was placed on baby food diet. I regained my health in a very short time, but being in northern Michigan in winter was a stressful time for me. We were still very much in love and *happy* with each other. There was so *little* for me to do after being so active on the farm, so I cleaned our home from one end to the other every single day. There was no dust *anywhere*; and as you can imagine in such a small space, when something was out of place, the whole space seemed confusing.

1e: Our Second Home

We were in Clare for a number of months, and when spring broke, Dean was transferred back to Port Huron. We traded in our small trailer for a 30-foot model. It seemed so *spacious* at first, after being so confined. We moved it to a lot in a park in our hometown and settled in again. This time, our home had a bathroom and a shower, and we felt really *rich* now. We had beautiful metal white cupboards in the kitchen, and we had an apartment-size stove. There was a bedroom in the back and a living room in the front with the kitchen, and a bath and storage were in the middle. It was such an improvement over what we had been in, and we felt very blessed indeed. We continued to attend Church and love the Lord as much as we knew how to. Our understanding was very limited, and we saw the Lord as more of a judge and punisher than one of love and mercy.

We began, by now, to long for a baby. I was still young, pushing 18, but I really longed for a child. I really wanted a boy, but Dean said he did not care. I finally went to my family doctor to see what was wrong, and he just laughed at me and said, "When you hit 18 and you are not pregnant, then come back; we will do some tests." Needless to say, it wasn't very long before I was pregnant. I suffered

16

a great deal of morning sickness, and it lasted the full 9 months.

1f: And Baby Makes Three

I was told by my doctor that I could deliver naturally, but when the day came and I went into labor, it was a different story. I labored 36 hours with no progress, so at the last moment, I was taken into an emergency C-section. The baby was a boy, 7 lbs., 4 ounces, and 21 inches long. To us, he was beautiful, and we named him Benny Dean Smith after his dad. He had big blue eyes, and he was so good-natured. He would spend *hours* just playing and talking, and he really didn't demand *holding* very much. He made our lives complete, and he wasn't very old when we had him dedicated to the Lord. We knew that the Lord had given him to us, and we wanted to give him back to God to use however he chose to.

We loved our Benny, but everything gets *smaller* with a wee one, and our little home was being pressed for space. There was only one small bedroom, and we had his crib in the corner. It was easy to tell that the room would not hold a full-size crib.

We began to house-hunt. We had no money for a down payment, and we knew that it would have to be *humble* so we could afford the payments. We located one outside the city a little ways. It had a deep well and a very run-down garage, and the house was painted a county road yellow, but we saw potential. It had two bedrooms, a kitchen, a living room, a bathroom with no tub, and a small utility room in the back off the kitchen. It was heated with a space heater in the living room, so many corners were cold as well as the floors. It came all furnished for $4800.00, and the payments were the right size.

We bought it, and after we began to move in and move things around, we discovered that, behind some of the furniture and under the cupboards, there were some very large *holes* in the walls. It was obvious they were not mouse-size, but *rat-size*. It was a *shock*, to say the least, because we had a 5-month-old baby. I was very concerned about him being bitten, and I would lie in our bed at night and listen to the rats over our heads running; and I would pray very hard that God would protect our child. It took a number of weeks and months before we had all the holes plugged, and I had lot more peace at night. The previous tenants had stood on the back step and had just thrown all the tin cans they used out behind in a huge pile. We loaded up all that trash and hauled it to the dump, and that got rid of a lot of hiding-and-feeding places for the rats.

We wallpapered a lot of the rooms and painted others. We laid new floors in the kitchen and put in a tub in the bathroom. We bought a washer for the utility room and patched holes in the walls in there with tin-can lids. We set out poison every night, and little by little, we defeated the problem. The last thing we did was to get a cat and confine her under the house. We gave her lots of milk and water, and she caught the rest of them. It was an enormous job, but we worked steadily and conquered the problem. We even painted the outside of the house white with green trim. We put down a carpet in the living room, hung curtains, and just in general made it our own home. The floors were not good, so Dean braced them with cement blocks and made them solid.

1g: Here Comes Penny

I got pregnant for our second child about that time. I couldn't believe it, as Benny was only 6 months, and I was having morning sickness again. I really struggled mentally with having another baby so soon, and I know that I did not help our little daughter along very well with my thoughts. You see, when we are carrying our children, it is very important what we are thinking.

Penny was born as a very upset, colic-ridden child, and I now know that I was responsible for a lot of that. I really was *rejecting* her throughout the entire pregnancy. I was fearful of the surgery and all the pain that it would bring. I just didn't feel ready for another baby at all. Nevertheless, she arrived on October 15, 1957, weighing 8 lbs., 4 oz., and 20 inches long. She was so round, and she had the most beautiful strawberry-blonde hair. We thought she was wonderful. That is, until we got her home.

Every night, she would scream from 2:00-3:00 a. m. until 7:00 or 8:00 a.m. Then, we would feed her and bathe her, and we would finally get some peace for a while. She acted like she was tormented, and I now feel that she was. I think she suffered with *rejection* from my mental processes while I was carrying her, and she did not know if anyone loved her. She suffered with projectile vomiting, and yet she gained weight easily. I went to my mother's for a couple of weeks until I could easily lift the baby and make some headway with healing of the incision.

When I returned home, she developed the croup, and Benny ended up with an ear infection, and they both were crying at the same time. My mother showed up one day and said, "Let me take the baby home while you deal with Benny and his ears." I was just so grateful. I was so worn out from the surgery, the constant crying, and the cleaning of the bottles: In those days, we *sterilized* the bottles and made formulas, etc. I had taken the children to the doctor, but it takes *time* to destroy infection and relieve pain.

Life became very *busy* with a newborn and a 15-month old, and there was no place for me to have time to think, pray, or anything. About this time in our lives, there wasn't a whole lot of praying going on anyway. I was young and foolish, and I thought that I could do everything on my own strength. Oh, how *foolish* I was: I had a lot to learn as well as Dean. We were walking in all that we knew spiritually, but most of the time, it was a life of worry, fear, and defeat.

My mother kept Penny for about 10 days, and she, later, told me that she sat up and held her night after night: Penny was strangling in her own mucous, and she would choke so hard that my mother believed that she (Penny) would have *died* if she (the mother) had not held her. When she choked, my mom would hear her, and she would go into action to help her. Penny was being treated with vaporizer medicine, etc., but it takes time for it all to dry up. She survived, and we brought her home.

The children seemed to be sick a lot in that little house. The floors were cold with the space heater, and Benny suffered with a bout of pneumonia while we lived there. I remember well, during our time there, how *isolated* I felt. We had only one car, and Dean was on transfer again, and I was alone with the children. We had a phone, but little else. My mom was a Godsend to me at that time. She would come and help me out a lot by buying milk, etc. for me. I was very nervous most of the time, and didn't really know what peace was.

Dean was transferred to Harbor Beach, Michigan. That was only about an hour-and-a-half from our home in Port Huron. It meant a lot of driving again. Harbor Beach is a nice little town on Lake Huron, and so Dean and I decided to take the children and live there for the short time that he would be located in that area. Penny was still a baby then, and Benny was a toddler. We found an upstairs apartment in an older home, all furnished and clean. We moved in and got settled. There were really huge old trees around the house, and the yard was beautiful. It was late spring and summer, and it was a really nice place to be.

We had come home to Port Huron for the weekend to visit parents, and we were returning back to Harbor Beach on a Sunday evening. Penny always had to go to bed early. She was a child that would go to bed early and get up early. It was her bedtime, and she was in her car seat. She began to get fussy and tired, and I tried everything to keep her quiet, but to no avail. She began to wail and cry with all her might. We were coming through a small town that was notorious for speed traps. Dean was going too fast, for he couldn't stand Penny crying so loud; and needless to say, we were pulled over and ticketed for speeding. All Penny wanted was to sleep in her own bed. The minute we laid her in her bed, she went right off to sleep.

We were back in Port Huron for a time when Dean was transferred to Cleveland, Ohio. Again, he wanted us with him. The children were small, just babies, and Danny had not come on the scene yet. Dean located an apartment in an old house. It had one large bedroom, sitting room combination, a kitchen, a bathroom, and a laundry in the basement. We hung up blankets to separate the children's sleeping quarters from ours. We had taken the crib for Penny, and Benny slept on a cot. It was not the best, but we could afford it, and it was clean and bug-free. It was always for only a short time, and we could take *anything* for a short time.

I was very confined there: The babies were small, the rooms few, and it was hard to fill my days with anything creative. Our spiritual lives at this time were almost zero, and I don't remember attending Church in Cleveland. Penny became very ill while we were there, and we had to find a doctor. She had developed some kind of an infection, and so we asked some people in the building where we could go for medical help. I remember it being evening, and we all were sitting in a doctor's office that would take her. She got the help she needed, and she became well again. We were there about 3 months, and another transfer came to go back home. So, homeward bound we happily became. We were traveling home with the crib tied to the top of the car, the trunk filled to the brim, and any extra space also taken with babies and all the things that entails. We were so glad to be heading home, and once again, Dean became a little heavy-footed. Pretty soon, along came a policeman and signaled us to stop. He asked why we were in such a hurry, and Dean explained about our being sent home after 3 months in Cleveland. The man took one look at the crib and the babies, and God gave us mercy: We were only warned -- Oh, the mercy of God.

1h: House-hunting Again

We soon became restless for a larger house, and so we began to look. We found one in the city with a small backyard, three bedrooms, a bath, living room, a good-sized kitchen, and a small utility room. We purchased it and began to move in. It was a brand-new Ranch style home, but it was not finished. We fenced in the yard, put aluminum windows on, seeded the lawn, and a year or so later, we built a nice two-car garage with room for a workbench on the end. We painted, hung curtains, and put on plastic tile in the bathroom to protect the wall from the shower.

Once again, I began to throw up in the mornings. I knew right away that I was pregnant again. I really was surprised this time, as we were trying to be so careful and all that, but God had a different idea.

Again, I was not really thrilled about having another child. It seemed that I had just gotten the other two where they were not sick all the time, and I felt that I had a handle on things, etc., but we don't always get what we think we want. In the plan of God, along came Danny.

1i: Child #3 Arrives

Danny was born on December 10, 1959. He weighed in at 9 lbs., 3 ounces, and it seems that he was 20 or 21 inches long. He was a very round little fellow. So now, I had a newborn, a 26-month old, and a 3½-year-old to take care of, which meant that one child was in diapers all the time, one in diapers at night, and the remaining one was pretty much potty-trained. I was busy.

Dean was working nearby and he was home every night. I really was not very happy at this time. I was home all the time, and I got out only to grocery shop and go to Church three times a week. Two of those times, we had the children with us, and on Wednesday nights, we hired a sitter, as we sang in the choir. We were not victorious Christians, and we felt no spiritual strength most of the time. Everyone that we knew was in the same boat, so we didn't question whether there was something more.

I did a lot of cooking, cleaning, baking, sewing all the clothes for the children, etc. Many times, Dean would come home from work, eat his supper, and want to go fishing every night in good weather. I really was frustrated, because I had three babies to bathe and get to bed on top of their care all day, and I needed the break. In those days, the woman didn't say a lot about how she felt. I finally, one night, spoke up and said that I really needed some help, and I would appreciate him helping me with their baths. Then, he could go fishing. He helped me willingly and then went to enjoy himself. I held *in* a lot of my feelings, as I would not have been a good wife or a good "Christian" if I had said what I really wanted to. How strange our ideas are sometimes about expressing what is the truth of our feelings. Where do we *learn* these things?

1j: School Years Begin

When it was time for Benny to start the kindergarten, the place we were living was just a little over 2 blocks from the school that he would be attending. It was a time when we did not worry over our children being taken and misused, and so he would walk it every day. At first, I accompanied him, but soon he knew his way very well, and he would do it all by himself. He really handled school beginnings very well.

Dean arrived home one night with the news that he was being transferred to Fort Scott, Kansas. He only had a short time before he had to report for work there. I was disappointed at the distance that he would be away from home, but I did understand that his job could send him to anywhere that he was needed. We talked about my going with him and then decided that, with Benny in school, it would not be wise to move the children that far. The decision was made for me to remain in Port Huron, and he would leave by himself.

He had purchased me an old car from my parents' neighbor in the country, so I did have transportation while he was away. The car was so old that it had no heater in it. It was faithful, though, to get me where I needed to go.

1k: Kansas, Here We Come

Dean left for his new assignment, and the children and I began to adjust to his absence. He would write and call me, of course, and we had a good marriage, but the children and I missed him terribly. Dean had been gone for a few weeks when I decided to join him. I would put Benny in a school there, and at least, we would all be together.

33

My mother told me that, with Danny being so little, it would be an awful job for me to tend to 3 children alone on a train for the length of time that it would take to travel so far. She said that she would keep Danny until I could get settled in out there, and then we could come home on a weekend to pick him up. I agreed to the plan. I purchased our tickets and told Dean when I would arrive. I had packed a few boxes of things and sent them ahead by Greyhound Bus, as I needed some articles to make wherever I was going a little homey.

I decided that we would use our camping materials that we had always used when we took the children on vacation. We had sleeping bags, metal dishes, and all the sturdy things that we had bought for such purposes. They would travel well, and of course, I sent blankets, bedding, towels, silverware, etc.

Dean had looked around for an affordable place where we could all live, and he was more than happy for our coming to be with him. He had done his best to provide a place for us.

The trip was very long, and with the two children, it was very tiring. I had to connect to other trains a few times, which meant hauling luggage and children from one train to another. When we arrived, we were exhausted, and Dean looked so wonderful to us. He was more than happy to see us, for it had been lonely for him without us.

He took us to the place that he had rented. Meanwhile, our boxes had arrived, and he had them in the apartment waiting for us. The apartment was only one big room with a bath and a kitchen. We hung clotheslines and hung blankets to separate the space for some privacy. We settled in and seemed to be adjusting to the lack of space fairly well. Once, I

35

noticed some powder along the wall in the kitchen, and I was suspicious about it. Why was it there? What was *wrong* with this place? We soon found out. I began to cook three meals a day, and then, it was no mystery as to why the powder was there. The place had *roaches*.

One day, I cooked a roast of beef in my electric frying pan, and all afternoon, as it roasted, every time I went to the kitchen, I would see them on the walls. I was a *wreck*, and my nerves were screaming all the time that we were there. We began to look for another place to live, for those conditions were intolerable. We found a place in a motel that had suites of rooms for rent. We had a living room, bedroom, kitchen, bathroom, and a room that connected to our bedroom, which was like an empty storage room. We used that for the children to sleep in.

The rooms were clean, well maintained, and roach-free. It was a very pleasant place for us, even though we were cramped for space. The people that we rented from were very pleasant, and so we got along. My nerves settled down, and we all seemed to be at a greater peace.

We soon missed our baby Danny so much that we decided to travel home to Port Huron on a Friday night as soon as Dean got out of work and pick him up. We put the two kids in the car and started out. We had not traveled very far when Benny became carsick. We were taken by surprise, for he had never had this problem before. It was all over the back seat, and as I remember, we took the car down to a stream nearby and did our best to clean things up. The car was a bit aromatic afterward, but we just kept going.

We traveled all night to reach Michigan. We did not have much time to stay in town, as we needed to get back on the road for the long trip back to Kansas.

We picked Danny up, spent a few hours with the family, and got back in the car for the long trip home. Dean had to be at work early that Monday morning, so there was nothing to do but keep driving. We took turns with the car and looking after the children, but everyone was so tired of moving. I remember getting out of the car to change drivers, and I was so dizzy that it felt like I was still in a moving car. We were very glad to get back to our little motel home in Fort Scott.

We had found a Church to attend. The pastor's name was Pastor Craven, and he would say that he was craven for souls to be saved; and he was. He had a fire in him, and we enjoyed his preaching very much. I think we actually had a bit more victory there in our lives than we had previously. The children seemed to be happy there as well.

After a short time there, Dean got transferred to Independence, Kansas. It was only a few miles from Fort Scott, and so we packed up the car, the kids, and us; and on we traveled, for the search for housing was upon us again.

We located a house trailer in Independence. After looking at so many dirty places, this seemed okay. We moved in and got settled, and when we started to cook again, out they came. This time they were *red* roaches, and I believe they are called German Roaches. I didn't care *what* they were called; I was a nervous wreck all over again. We had put Benny in kindergarten there, and he was actually doing quite well in making the adjustment to a new place and a new school.

It was an extremely lonely, confusing time for us. We knew that we could not stay in the trailer, as none of us could stand the roaches. We sprayed and did all we could, but we have never lived with that kind of setting, and it was intolerable. So again, the search was on for another home.

We looked in the small paper there and made many calls. It took a lot of looking, and we heard many *"We don't want children"* before we finally found a place to hang our hats. I remember reading an ad in the paper and making a call to answer an ad for an apartment in an older house. The man that answered was really drunk, for his words were slurring, but he knew what I was saying. I asked if he allowed children, and he said, "I don't care how many children you have, as long as you take care of the place." We looked at it, and it was *spotless*. It had a really good-size kitchen, a large living room, a good-size bedroom, a big bathroom, and a huge closet.

We bedded the older two down in the living room in their sleeping bags, and in the huge closet, we placed a folding cot with Danny on it. We had our privacy there in that apartment; and again, Benny was placed in another school. What a challenge for a five-year-old to have.

One more time we settled in, and wonder of wonders, there were no roaches! While we lived there, Benny hurt his head on the monkey bars at school, and it required stitches to fix him up. It was over his eye, and the teacher called me to tell me that he needed to be picked up for some care. I called Dean, and he left work to pick him up at school. We all went to the hospital, for the stitches needed to close up the wound. He was a real little trooper about it, and he didn't cry at all. We stayed in that apartment until Dean was transferred back to Port Huron. It was a good place to be for us.

11: Another New Home

It was an extremely busy time again in our lives. Benny was in the kindergarten; Penny was 3½; and Danny was about 16 months old when we began to want to get out of our home in the city. We wanted some property outside of town where the kids could have more space to play without our worrying about the busy street with its heavy traffic. Our dream grew, but we had no money again. It took every dime to keep together what we had, for we were a one-income family. Sometime later that year, we began to look for something that would accommodate us better.

We found a really nice home a few miles outside the city. It was in a nice section with a little over an acre of land, and the house was wonderful.

42

It had three very large bedrooms, a bath-and-a-half, all hardwood floors, a kitchen that was every woman's dream, a really large living room, a nice-size utility room, and a huge walk-in attic. Every place where there was a nook or cranny, there was a *storage cupboard* of some kind. There was a large pantry off the kitchen, a large double car garage, half of the driveway was cement, and it had a beautiful yard that was large enough for a ball field. We fell in love with the place, and after a few things fell into place, it was ours.

We were so excited. We moved in November of 1961, and we had our family Thanksgiving that year in the new place. Benny had to be taken out of the old school and put into the kindergarten of the new school, and that was a huge adjustment for him. After all, he had been in 4 schools for his first year.

1m: Another Transfer

We moved in November, and in January, Dean had to go to Missouri on transfer. I was left alone with 3 children in a new house that I did not know at all. I had an old car, so I could get to the store, etc., but I was in a new neighborhood where I didn't know anybody.

The first thing that happened, after Dean left for Missouri, was that we had a very cold night, and the wind blew hard all night. I got up in the morning and used the upstairs bathroom, and no water came back in when I flushed the toilet. I realized that the water had frozen up during the night, and I had three children to get off to school. I sure did need a plumber.

I managed to get the children off to their classes, and then I telephoned a plumber who attended our Church. He came out and replaced a large section of copper tubing under the house that had frozen and split. He got everything flowing again and told me that the vents under the house were open, and that was why the pipe had frozen up. He closed the vents, and I had no more problems with pipes freezing ever again.

While Dean was gone on transfer, I took one room at a time and painted all the way through. I then varnished all of the beautiful birch woodwork and cupboards as well as painting the inside of all the cupboards with white enamel. It kept my mind off the loneliness that I felt, with Dean so far away. We were writing all the time, but it was very hard on both of us to be apart so long.

We loved our new home and all of its space. It was so wonderful. We built a ball diamond in the back, erected a swing set, and built-and-filled a sand box. Most of the time, the neighborhood children were playing in our yard. The kids had bicycles and a basketball hoop on the garage, and so we were always having lots of activity around our home.

At this time, we switched from a Church called Ross Memorial Church to the Wadhams Baptist Church, and we never missed a meeting. We paid our tithes and helped out where we could. We were typical good Christians without a clue as to the real power or reality of a living God.

We were both living very non-victorious lives as to overcoming a lot of habits, vices, and language, but most of all, we had no patience or love in many instances. When I look back, I wish that I knew *then* what I know *now*, for I would have raised the children very differently. We cannot go back, and we need not feel guilty about our lack of many things *then*. There is no guilt in where we were;

there is only ignorance of knowing the truth. We worked in all that we knew at the time.

Chapter 2: Doing Too Much

2a: Connie Goes to Work

By this time, the children were getting older, and so I went out to work. I had not finished high school, as I married after the tenth grade. I attended a number of evening courses and then took the tests for the GED diploma and passed. I then proceeded to take a number of courses in office practice, bookkeeping, etc. Remember, these were the days before computers, and so everything was done the old-fashioned way. God always blessed me with the ability to manage many things that were above my level of schooling, and I thank him that I had a good mind and could learn quickly.

I held a job handling government contracts for tank sprockets. A sprocket is just like a tire on a car. The sprocket drives the tank, and when they wear out or break, there is a tank sitting and going nowhere. It was very detailed work, and I loved it. The contracts ran out, and so did the job.

Then, I went to work at a propane gas company. It ended up being 9 hours a day, 6 days a week. I would go home drained completely. I had to sell the items, bill the customers, take the calls for orders, handle a two-way radio to dispatch messages to the men in the trucks, do all the accounting, clean the bathroom, make the coffee, make the deposits, etc. I had 3 children at home, a large house to keep clean, a husband that needed my attention, and 3 meetings a week at a Church that gave me no strength spiritually.

I was very, very particular about the cleanliness of our home. It was in the days when the woman was supposed to be perfect in every department: She was to be a great cook, a tremendous sex partner, a perfect mother, keep an immaculate house, hold a full-time job, always have the laundry caught up, and most of all, make homemade nutritious meals for the family. It was an unwritten law somewhere in the unknown, and we all tried to follow it either consciously or subconsciously. It put a tremendous strain on me to keep this unwritten law.

On many Sunday mornings, I would be so weary from the week that I didn't feel like going to Church. I felt like getting ahead of all the work and staying home to do so. The guilt-trip was too large, so I usually managed to attend Church, even though

I slept through many sermons because they were so dead. Nobody ever knew if anyone was there in their spirit.

2b: Diet-pill Disaster

This was a time in our world when the rainbow diet pills were the rage. If you don't know what I mean, I would take a blue pill before breakfast, a red one before lunch, a green one before supper, a laxative pill to keep you emptied out, etc. It was all the rage, and I always suffered with too much weight, so I became one of the many who chose that way to lose the weight and keep it off. I had no idea what I was doing to my physical body: After all, I had to see a doctor to get them, so I assumed they were safe.

What they really were, I learned later, were uppers, downers, and laxatives. I was pretty much working the clock around, because they gave me so much energy. Finally, one day, I became very depressed and developed a cough. I called my family doctor and went to see him. Meanwhile, for the first time in my life, I was at the correct weight for my height (according to the charts). Anyway, after examining me, the doctor found that I was dehydrated and depressed. I had taken the pills to show him what I was taking, and he really became angry and told me to stop them immediately. He put me on anti-depressants, and I left the job to get well. I had pushed myself into a nervous breakdown. I took his pills and slept the clock around. My mom came and took our children, as I was unable to care for them.

2c: Descend into Depression

It was a very dark time for all of us. My husband would drive 1½ hours to get to his job, work 8 hours, and drive the same length of time home to find a wife on the couch sleeping. He had to make the dinner and get the kids ready for bed, etc., as I was useless. I had no idea that God could set me free. I was depressed for quite a few months. I finally got well enough so that when another job was offered to me, I felt well enough to take it.

I went to work for an appliance dealer in our town. I did the bookkeeping, billing, sold TVs, washers, dryers, refrigerators, etc., answered the phone, kept track of the repairmen, and many times held down the whole store so the boss and owner could go golfing. I worked from 9:00-5:30 each day for 5 days a week.

Eventually, I felt that I was under the same old strain with work, kids, house, Church, husband, and all the invisible perfections that society had placed on me. I never felt good enough for God, and I always felt that I fell short of his levels of perfection.

53

My husband was suffering the same feelings, but I did not know that he was. We never talked about our spiritual thoughts, just the regular mundane money problems, children problems, work-needed-around-the-house stuff of everyday life. We did our best to pray with our children and read Bible storybooks to them. Each morning before work and school, I would read a daily devotional to them and pray over breakfast, but it all was so shallow and meaningless. It was merely actions without spirit or love to it. Thank God that was soon to change.

My health suffered again, and I had to leave my job again to stay home and get well. It was my nerves once more, and I remained home about 9 months, this time, before returning to the appliance store. I only worked another 6-9 months, and I knew that I needed to be home. I stayed home for quite a length of time with the children. Even though they were getting older, my daughter told me that she was glad that I was home when they got out of school, for it gave her a sense of security.

Chapter 3: Call From God

3a: How Willing Are You?

It was about this time, suffering yet from depression, that I heard God say to me one day, "How long are you going to stay in that pit?" I said, "I didn't know I had a choice." He said, "It is all up to you. You can get out anytime you choose." I took a new look at the situation and decided to stop taking my tranquilizers. I began to feel better, and little by little, I climbed out of the pit of depression that I had been in for years. I am very careful now, and I watch my thinking closely. If I begin to think negative, or if everything looks dark, I begin to praise the Lord: I cannot stay negative while I'm praising him. There is so much to praise him for. Just look around you, and you will see that you, too, have much to be grateful for.

About this time, I went out to work again, this time with an accountant. I had a number of jobs that I was responsible for, and a lot of my work was with payrolls. I had worked there for quite a few months when I got up one morning and didn't feel well, so I stayed home.

I lay on the couch and read a book that I had been wanting to read, *"Through Gates of Splendor."* It was the story of the martyred missionaries in South America. I heard the voice of the Spirit say to me, "These people were this willing. How willing are you"? Over and over, this message came to me. Finally, I said, "God, I have given you my children; I have given you my home; and I have given you my life. I have given you *everything* I own. I don't know what you *want* of me?" He said, "I want your job."

Immediately, I thought of what my husband would think, for we really needed the money. We had the typical handful of payment books like everyone else, and we needed every dime we made. Nevertheless, I had heard God's voice, and there was no mistaking it. When Dean came home that night and supper was over, I told him my story. His response was wonderful, for he said, "If that is what God wants, then that is what we will do." I gave my two-week's notice the next day. I wept when I told the boss my story, and he said, "I hope you find what you are looking for." I replied, "I know I will."

3b: Another Church, Same Thinking

We had changed Churches again, but we still were in the Baptist mind-set, and the Church that we were attending was another Baptist one. Again, we were doing all the things that we felt were required of us: attending every meeting, paying our tithes, helping out to maintain the Church, and singing in the choir. We had switched Churches because we had felt very *stifled* in the last one. It seemed to us that the message was, "One of the only people that were somehow going to make it, were the *Baptists*." We questioned our pastor on it, and my husband made a stand in the yearly meeting: He said that he felt like he was being brainwashed. The pastor called us to a meeting, and when we confronted him on our thoughts in the matter, he told us that we should leave. He was a very sick man, and he was not a true pastor, for he had no love or caring for the people.

How do some of these so-called men of God think that they should be pastors? They would be better off doing something completely *different* than dealing with people's lives.

We were pretty content in the new Church, but still, there was not much growth in our lives spiritually. Dean felt weak in his faith on the job, and I felt about the same. I kept busy with cleaning, laundry, sewing, lawn work, cooking, and baking all kinds of good things and freezing them. I also canned tomatoes and made homemade relish, pickles, and chili sauce. And with the Church activities, I kept busy all the time.

3c: The Wind of the Spirit

In 1971, our lives changed radically, and all because of what our daughter Penny had experienced at camp. She was at camp for only a week, but it was long enough to change her entire life.

As the girls were around the campfire one night, many of them witnessed a life-changing experience: The Spirit of God swept into the campground. The Holy Spirit became so real that many of the girls were deeply stirred and filled with the Holy Spirit. There was so much weeping and such a sense of God's presence that Penny came home asking many questions about the power of the Spirit. Her first question was, "What is the Holy Spirit?"

As Baptist people, we had heard of Father God and, of course, his son Jesus Christ; but we had heard very little about the *third* person of the Trinity, the Holy Spirit. When Penny asked her question, we gave our usual Churchy answers such as, "The Holy Spirit is the third person of the Trinity," etc., but we could not explain what is meant by the *baptism* of the Spirit. We really felt that we had no answer for her, but it was very obvious that she was deeply stirred.

It was the catalyst to get us both thinking. If there was another experience that one could have that would make God real and give more power, we needed it badly. I really feel that *that* was what God used to ignite the fire under us to open our minds to more. We had a salvation experience when we were young, and our children had all met the Lord at a young age, but none of us were trying to let Christ rule us in any way.

It was in September, just a couple of months after Penny's experience at camp when we were in a prayer meeting on a Wednesday night. The usual procedure in our Church was that only one person prayed at a time. We were in a small side room for the meeting, and it was a warm night for the time of year. I heard God say to me, "If you open your mouth tonight, you will receive something wonderful." Along with these words, I had the greatest anticipation overwhelm me, and I could hardly wait for the person praying to finish.

When I began to pray, I had the most awesome feeling overwhelm me. It felt like someone had taken a large pitcher of warm honey and had poured it all over me. I prayed the strangest prayer, for I prayed and said, "Lord, it is not warm in here from the weather; it is warm in here because of your love."

The pastor's wife had gone somewhere some weeks before, and she had received the baptism of the Spirit. She was sitting in front of me, and as I was praying, she reached around and squeezed my hand. That was my moment of a tremendous turnaround in my life. I finished my prayer, and when the meeting was over, I heard God say to me, "You can help." He, then, named a friend that I had been speaking to earlier that week about some marriage problems that she was having. I went to her right away and said that I could help her. We set a time and date right then. Later, when I spoke to her, she was helped, and her marriage improved. Again, I had no idea as to what I had received and the radical change that it would make in my life.

It was common for all the younger couples to get together and go out to eat somewhere on Saturday nights. The following Saturday night, we crossed over the Blue Water Bridge and went to Canada for their famous "Fish and Chips." We had a good time, and we decided to come back to our home for fellowship.

One of the couples was acting so strange. The man kept going to the door, look out, and pace around. He seemed highly *agitated* over something, and we knew that God was working on him. He and his wife finally left for their own home, and eventually everyone left.

We went to pick up our daughter, who was babysitting at one of the couple's home. When we went in, another one of the men (who had received the baptism) came in too, and he sat across from our daughter and told her how to receive the Holy Spirit's power. We watched our daughter's face light up with a heavenly glow, and as she received, Dean thought, "If it is that easy, then I want it too," and he received as well. It was a shouting, mind-changing night, and we were never the same again.

When we arrived home, our phone rang, and it was the couple that had left early. They were calling to let us know that the man had thrown himself on his knees beside his bed and had surrendered himself to God. It was an amazing time for all of us Baptists to really come alive for the first time.

We went to Church and stood and wept over the old hymns, as they had meaning for the first time. We had so much joy, and the people could see it. When they asked us what had happened, we told them boldly, and they said that they already had it. No one can help those that need no help. We would praise the Lord and clap our hands when we worshipped, and that was not done in our Church.

We had been leading the youth group for some time, and when we received this wonderful experience, we shared it with the youth. We had been holding the group in our home, and we had as many as 40 young people in our home at each meeting. They began to go home and get on their knees and receive the baptism of the Holy Spirit. Then they would boldly tell their parents that they were speaking in other tongues as the Scripture says.

Needless to say, when God moves so powerfully, there is always someone to get unhappy or not understand, and so it was with this as well. We were visited by the deacons. They said that we were being *offensive* with our joy and that we could never understand.

Then, our pastor asked us to stop teaching the baptism of the Holy Spirit, and we said that we could not do that: We must tell the truth, and that is the truth. We were told that we had to bring the group back into the Church, and we said that we couldn't do that, as we would lose the kids. Then, we made a compromise: We would keep the group through the end of the school year (of 1972). We, later, had a pizza party at our home; and we turned in our keys and dropped the group.

The parents were not happy, as their teens did not want to go to Church anymore. We could not help that, as we were unable to keep them in their newfound liberty.

Shortly after, the pastor began to preach against those who were still participating in our cause, claiming that we were *conjuring up* the Spirit. We were doing no such thing! The pastor had not received the baptism of the Spirit, and he did not understand what we were doing when we gathered. The Spirit was *already* there in each one of us, and it didn't *need* any conjuring up. Our pastor was very *threatened* by what was happening, and he felt that he was losing control. It made it impossible for us to stay, and so we began to seek where we now belonged.

We are grateful to God for using that pastor to push us on, for it was the best thing that he could have ever done for us.

3d: The Search for Truth

Our search for truth began in the late summer of 1972. We went to a small independent Church, and on our first Sunday there, the Church *split*, so it was obvious that this particular Church was not for us. Next, we visited an *"Assembly of God"* Church. They told us that we had not received the baptism of the Spirit, as we did not speak in tongues the right way. We knew what we had received, for we had power for the first time in our lives. I immediately received discerning of spirits, prophecy, and the interpretation of tongues; and we had love, peace, joy, etc., and there was a 180-degree turn in our lives.

Then, went to a *"Church of God."* They didn't agree with our method of receiving either, but God told us to stay there. We attended for quite some time and led a teen Sunday school class. Young people were being saved, but the old-timers were not happy about it. For the Spirit-filled people, there was no joy or love, and we seemed to *annoy* them with our joy. We had some wonderful experiences while we were there. Then, one Wednesday night in the spring of 1974, I was in prayer meeting, and I heard God say, "What are you doing here?" I didn't say anything until we were in the car. I asked Dean if he had heard anything in the meeting. He said "Yes": He had heard the same thing that *I* had heard. That was the end of our Church-going, for God said, "Go home and teach your own children." So we proceeded to do just that.

3e: Home-Church Begins

Before we even began, we received a phone call, asking us if we were starting a new Church. We said, "Not really. We were just going to hold meetings in our home for our own family." The caller asked if they, along with some others, could be a part of that, and we said "Yes." We ended up with about 15 people the first week. We would literally move out pieces of furniture from our living room and set up folding chairs and a small podium, and we did that for 3 meetings a week. Apparently, we must have thought that we had to stay with the traditional times, for that is what we did. The group continued to grow until we had 20-25 members, and we said that we had to look for a *building*, as our home was getting very full.

3f: We Outgrow the Home

We found a small store nearby that was empty. It had a main part and a small back room, which would do for a Sunday school room for the teens, as we seemed to have a good group of them. It had neither water nor sewer in it, so we rented a Porta-Pottie and carried in a jug of water for drinking. We had a lawn to mow and the place to keep clean. We brought the small podium and the chairs from the house, and when we needed more chairs, we bought them little by little. We built a small platform, etc. and made it our own.

3g: Our First Minister

We had a woman living near us who was Spirit-filled with a tremendous gift for the word, and she preached and taught us for quite a few months. She was wonderful, and she taught us how to move in the gifts of the Spirit; and we will always be grateful for her in our lives at that time. Her husband finally did not want her to be gone every Sunday, as he was a truck driver and had very few days off. He wanted to spend time with her, and he asked her not to preach anymore. So she left us.

As far as qualifications go, we had a gentleman in our midst who was next in line to take over the preaching. So he stepped in and became our new minister. He was blind in the natural, and so it was very difficult for him to research a message. He did his best, but he was very limited.

He served us in the role as minister for 3-6 months. (The sister had been with us about 6 months.) In that time, Dean and I were growing and hungering after the Spirit. I was sitting in the meeting one Sunday morning, and as our blind brother was preaching, I heard my Spirit man say to me, "Feed me, I am dying in here." I sought the Lord for food for my Spirit, and he said, "Study the Tabernacle of Moses."

I got books and studied them, and it fed me so much. I was the Sunday school teacher for the teens, and Dean was the Sunday school superintendent. After a week of teaching the teens on the Tabernacle, I said to Dean, "This teaching is for the whole

Church, not for just the teens." He said, "If that is what God wants, that is okay with me."

I began to teach the whole Church during the Sunday school time, and the reaction from the people was really very encouraging. They would come up to me after the service and say, "Where did you ever learn these things, for I am learning so much from this teaching?" I would explain just how the Lord had led me to teach the material that they were learning each week. I felt that I was truly hearing from the Lord, for the people were growing and learning so much. Little did I know just what was going on over the telephone behind our backs.

After a couple of months, one Sunday morning, our (blind) pastor got up and said, "If Dean will come forward, I would like him to read my resignation letter." So, Dean stepped forward, not having any idea as to what was going on. He read the resignation letter, whereupon the minister left the Church, and half of his supporters followed him. Needless to say, it was a great shock to all of us. We didn't know that there was a problem, but the minister must have been offended somehow. Dean announced from the pulpit that there would be a meeting there that night.

3h: God Calling

That day, in that little building, was our call into full-time work for the Lord, which was in late 1974. We had no idea of the vastness of the call of God that would carry us around the world. It was best that we *didn't* at that point.

We went home and fell on our knees, and we fasted and waited on God for what he wanted from us. We were the only ones that could possibly lead the group at that time. It was an awesome, overwhelming feeling when we were not looking for leadership, and it just *fell* on us. The Spirit of God has a way of doing that sort of thing without warning.

We felt such a great lack of training in the natural for what God was asking of us, but we knew that he would provide the training for us, and he certainly did do that. He was so gentle, loving, and supportive to us during the entire schooling in the Spirit time. We always say, "We did not go to *'theology'* school,' but we went to *'Kneeology'* School." We felt a complete dependence on God for everything. He always was faithful to supply whatever we needed, whether it was a message, finance, courage, faith, people, answers, etc. We felt very humbled by hearing his call, and we knew that we needed all the help that we could get.

That night, our first night after the minister's resignation, we held a meeting as usual. The Holy

Spirit was so kind to us. He swept into the meeting and began to speak to us through the prophetic word, through tongues and interpretation of tongues, and discerning of spirits. He really was the minister in every way. Everyone went home blessed, encouraged, strengthened, and helped in any area that they had a need.

From that night on, we had just one powerful move of the Spirit of God after another. He was truly a mother and a father to us in every way. We kept praying, fasting, and seeking his face, and he never failed us. I continued to teach the Tabernacle, and we kept up the meetings regularly as usual. When we looked around after the Church split, we realized that God had removed all the people that did not tithe or work in any way. We felt as the Scripture says: He, God, is the husbandman, and he prunes the things away that are not producing fruit, so the things that are left, can produce greater fruit.

3i: A New Meeting Place

That period lasted for about another six months. Then, we received notice from our landlord in the spring of 1975: They wanted us to vacate the building. They wanted to set up a business there that sold dog food, etc. Now, we were responsible for a group of people that had no meeting place.

We proceeded to search our town over, looking for the place that God would have us be next. Everything we looked at was too expensive, too small, had no parking space, etc. We looked at everything that came up, and then my mother called. She was in our group at that time, as well as my father, and she said that the old schoolhouse, called the *"Malane School,"* was empty, and we should go and look at it. We made arrangements to go through

78

it with the owner. The building was very old, about 100 years or so, and it had been used through the years for everything. Churches had been in there, diet clubs, and other meetings as well. No one ever really cared much about the old building, and it showed. We went through it all together: Dean and I, my parents, the owner. It had no electricity, no heat except for a huge old furnace, no water or sewer, and it was painted a mustard color on the top and hot pink on the bottom inside. It was worn-out white on the outside. What a sight it was!

We all came out of the building really feeling that it sure could not be the place, for the amount of work and money to fix it up would be *huge*. We thanked the owner and said that we would let him know. When the four of us talked, we said, "That can't be the place," and we all went to our respective homes and dropped it.

3j: The Work Begins

The next day, I heard the Lord say, "Go back, you missed it, that is my will for you in this matter." Well, we went back, spoke to the owner, and made him an offer for rent, and he *took* it. We began the very big job of converting what had become an eyesore into a very precious building for worship. Everyone in the group helped, and we *needed* everyone, for we had the inside and outside to completely renovate. We all gathered and began the huge job ahead of us. My husband completely renovated the electrical system. Dean and my dad did all the installing of outlets and a new fuse box, and then we called the Edison Company to re-hook up the power from outside. We drug out the old furnace and had a new under-the-floor forced-hot-air oil furnace installed in the building, with thermostat control. We bought an oil barrel and had it filled, and then we partitioned off some small Sunday school rooms and a small space for a nursery. We dropped the very high, old ceiling and installed lighting so we could all see to read the Bible.

Then we rented a paint sprayer; and when we began to spray the paint on the upper part of the room, the glory of the Lord hit us, and we began to praise him in English and in tongues. We painted the upper part a light beige, and the lower wainscoting part a dark brown. We had the place carpeted; even the *altar* was upholstered with carpet. My mother papered a small room in the back that had formerly held coal for the stove, and we made a small bathroom in that area. We purchased a Porta-Pottie like those for camping, and it was very attractive. We cleaned up the yard, for it was full of old branches, stones, and debris of all kinds. The previous tenants had just thrown all the junk out in the yard behind the building, so the backyard looked like a dump. After all of this was done, we built a sign to read what we believed. We called ourselves, "God's Way: Full Gospel."

That building, today, has been moved from its original location to another location in our town, a few miles away. It has been freshly painted and redone inside. It is being preserved as a kind of museum of one-room schools of the past. When we pass it, it brings back many wonderful memories of our years in it and all we learned during that time. It was truly, again, a spiritual education for us. One cannot learn in books what the Holy Spirit taught us there.

In any event, one of the lessons I personally learned in that place was one of humility. As mentioned above, we had to have a Porta-Pottie to serve as our bathroom, due to the fact that there was no piped-in water there. The building was very old, and water wasn't usually installed in the old one-room schools, for the toilets in those days were the outside variety. The Porta-Pottie had to be emptied, of course, and no one offered to do it. I waited and waited, but it just did not happen. Finally, common sense said, "Take it home and clean it out." Very grudgingly, I did just that. I was complaining to the Lord the entire time that I was doing the job. I said to him, "Why do I have to do it? I'm the pastor's *wife*." He said, "That is why you have to do it." We, as leaders in God's work, must always lead in every department, the *pleasant* and the *unpleasant*. I said, "Okay, Lord, if that is what I must do, I will do it with joy and not with resentment." After that, we made a joke about it: Every Wednesday night, after our meeting, we would go and get it, and as we carried it to the car, we would say, "Along came

John." It was still messy and smelly, but my attitude had changed, and so it was easier. I had accepted God's will for my life.

When we moved in (summer of '75), it was a completely different-looking building. The yard was neat, the parking lot was distinct and had new gravel, the sign was up, the lights were on, and the bathroom was usable and decent. We brought a jug of water every week, with paper cups, so if anyone needed a drink, it was available. We had a place for a pantry so we could help others in need; and in that space, we also had a small library. We had purchased a piano for the *first* building, and so we had that for music. We had made a Sunday school classroom in the back next to the bathroom where our son Benny taught a young class each week. Our daughter Penny taught some other children in one of the other classrooms, and we had the nursery in use at every meeting.

My father built a new podium for us as well as some bookshelves, and he made me a blackboard. Our son Benny and his wife Janet took it upon themselves to learn the guitar. They would play in every service, and they would lead the *singing* on occasion. I led the singing a lot and usually taught on Wednesday night. Dean usually preached on Sunday mornings, and our son Benny preached on Sunday night. Our lives were full, God was good, our lives were changing, and we felt happy and peaceful.

3k: God's Provision

We went to offer the landlord the first month's rent, and he said, "I cannot take that, because you people have done so much to improve the place that I cannot charge you rent." We, then, made a deal with him: We would provide a receipt every month for the amount of the rent to be used as a donation to the ministry, and he could use it on his taxes. He agreed, and so it was done. We never paid a single month's rent all the time that we were in that building. While we were fixing up the place, people would walk in and say, "What are you doing here?" When we told them, they often would donate money for us to use in the improvements. God was so good in the whole matter, and to think that we didn't think it was the place!

We learned so very much in this humble building. It was surely our training ground. Dean, our son Ben, and I came into our ministries in that place. Ben really began to come forth in his ability to minister the word, and he had a powerful anointing. We felt so very blessed to have him with us in the work of God, and we felt very proud of him when he was in the pulpit. We found out later, a bit *too* proud.

Chapter 4: Beginning of Our Overseas Ministries

4a: Our First Overseas Trip

After all of our hard work on the old building that God had chosen for us, we heard about a trip (in the fall of 1975) to the Holy Land that was being led by a local pastor and his wife. It would be a small group that was going, and if we would go, the minister and his wife could go for *free*. We had never considered traveling overseas, but we were being stirred up by God's Spirit to make this journey. We were informed of all the places that we would visit and how many days we would be gone;

and after praying about it, we felt that God would have us say "Yes." We applied for our passports and went to the meetings involved to inform us of how to travel overseas. We received a printed itinerary of where we would be and when, and we began to get excited about the whole experience.

We informed our Church of our plans, and they began to donate toward our trip; and we began to save for it as well. All in all, when the time came to make the proper deposits, etc., we had what was needed. We were told to dress up every day, which meant a lot of luggage. We gathered clothing and figured out what our needs would be in other areas, and we began to pack and grow more full of anticipation every day. Our Church would be in good hands while we were gone, as our son could preach extremely well, and the people loved him a lot.

We flew out of Detroit Metropolitan Airport, and all I can remember is that it was a long, long trip, and we had many layovers. I do remember well getting off in Brussels, Belgium, and *guns* were held on us as we disembarked from the plane. I saw that one of my suitcases had begun to pull apart at the seam, and my *panties* were hanging out. I asked if I could fix it, and they said, "Absolutely not." I prayed that I would have enough underwear when we arrived in Tel Aviv.

It was a 10-day trip, and our first few days in Jerusalem were in the YMCA. It was more than interesting, as there were *bullet holes* in the walls of a hotel, and we knew that they were evidence of a *battle* of some kind in that area. I remember walking the old streets of the old city where our Lord walked and thinking to myself, "Jesus actually stepped here where *I* am stepping," and it was an awesome feeling.

The next morning, bright and early, we started on our travels. We saw the valley where David slew Goliath; we went to the Wailing Wall; we saw the Dome of the Rock; and we visited many other areas in the next few days. We took a bus, of course, to these places, but when we approached some areas, we were told that we were not allowed to go there, for there was *gunfire* in that area. We could see the warfare on the Golan Heights. We traveled to Cana of Galilee, where Jesus turned water into wine, and we visited the upper room and had communion there. I did not feel that it was the real place, and I did not have any great presence sweep over me.

Many of the places where great things happened are so commercialized that we were disappointed. The Garden of Gethsemane was an amazing place for us: There was such a presence of God that came over us that we went aside from the group to just stand and praise the Lord. The olive trees that Jesus prayed under are there yet, as none have died or been cut down. They were *huge*, and if they could talk, it would be very interesting to hear what they would say.

We visited the site of Jesus' birth, and I did not feel anything there. There were *two* places where they said Golgotha was, and one was in the city, which would not be scriptural: They did not crucify *anyone* inside the city wall. The second spot for Golgotha was the one that we felt was the real one. We went to the empty tomb, and that was a very interesting spot. The walking was very difficult, for everything was uneven and rocky.

I became very ill with dysentery in Caesarea. In the morning, I did not dare to eat anything: The bathroom situation was not good, and I knew that I would be challenged throughout the day. When the others went down from their rooms to the restaurant, they asked if there was a doctor in the house; and there was. I was able to get some medication for the problem, but the inconvenience held on for 24-36 hours. I finally got well, which was a big relief.

We traveled to the Dead Sea area and saw Masada and a number of other places; and all in all, I felt that we really saw a lot in a few days. We went back to Tel Aviv to fly out; our next stop was Athens, Greece.

Athens was a very different kind of place. We saw the Parthenon and many statues, and we had a taxi ride with a very bad driver. He was going the wrong way on a one-way street, cursing in Greek at all the other drivers. God kept us safe for sure.

There must have been many angels camped all around us.

There was an older couple traveling with us. They would have been in there 70's if I remember correctly. The gentleman had suffered a heart attack some months before, and so his wife was a bit *concerned* about him and all the walking involved. The ground was very rough, and it was *rocky* everywhere we went. This couple was having a bit of trouble managing their footing, so Dean and I watched over them quite a bit.

When we arrived in Greece, we all were very tired, and we proceeded to get our rooms in the hotel where reservations had been made. Some of the group proceeded to lie down for a nap. The plan was for us all to meet at a certain time for our sightseeing and for dinner. When we assembled later, we learned that the older man had gone out on the street alone: He was looking for a newspaper. He saw a man and asked where he might find a paper, and the man said, "Follow me." The man led him to a house of prostitution. What a *shock* that was! The older man didn't understand what was happening when he was told to sit down and order some alcohol. The man refused to do that, and then a woman came out scantily dressed and proceeded to stand very close and be seductive with him.

The poor man was scared to death! He had no idea that, on the streets of Athens, Greece, when a man asked for a newspaper, it meant that he was looking for some physical action. Anyway, the man (who had led him there) became very angry, and there was much shouting in Greek. Ultimately, the older man was allowed to leave: He was almost physically *thrown* out of the place.

The older man didn't know where he was, for he had not paid enough attention to the location of the hotel or the location of the place where the man had led him. He was alone on the streets of Athens. He could not speak the language, and he didn't have a *clue* as to where the hotel was. Somehow, God led him back to the hotel, and we all later learned about this story. He returned white as a sheet, and his heart was beating like he was ready to have another attack. We, then, decided that no one would go out on the street alone again. The older man did recuperate enough to enjoy the sights of Athens and his supper.

We learned many things on that trip. One of them was that we would make our own arrangements from then on. Some of the details had not been properly taken care of, which left us in some pretty precarious places in foreign lands.

We were very glad to get back home after our 10 days overseas. Little did we know how many times we would do overseas flights in days to come. We had not yet received the worldwide vision that God would give us later. We do know that we learned a great deal on the trip, and we would use the wisdom that we gained to keep us safe on future journeys that God would open for us.

About this time, God began to move on Dean to become ordained. He fought pretty hard, as it was not his choice; it was *God's* choice. We had *no idea*, at that time, about all the traveling we would do in years to come. Titles are important to many people, but never were to us. Nevertheless, when God speaks, we listen; and sooner or later, we obey.

We decided to take a vacation for a week or so. Dean had some vacation time coming from his work, so we turned the Church over to our son, and we left.

We made a trip to Washington D.C., Virginia, etc. We had been gone for a few days when Sunday rolled around. We looked for a Church to attend, and we located one near our motel. We got up and dressed for the meeting, and we deliberately sat in the back of the Church. The minister of the Church walked right up to Dean, shook his hand, and said, "You are a minister, and God wants you to speak this morning." Dean almost fainted: He had been *running* from being ordained, and here we were in a completely strange place with a minister of God speaking the very words Dean did not want to hear. God always *confirmed* everything he has told us in one way or another. Dean did speak that morning, and he did very well. He knew in his heart that the running was now over for him.

Dean finally submitted to the will of God in the matter. We held an ordination service in that renovated one-room school, and it was glorious. Our son was being dealt with about being ordained as well, so it was a *double* ordination that evening. It was held on September 30, 1976. We had special singers and a special speaker, and most of all, we had a glorious presence of God to confirm what he had been asking. God led us on by his voice, by his word, through the Bible, and through prophecies as well.

4b: The Call to the Philippines

We heard of a meeting being held in Brighton, Michigan. It was in the late fall of 1976, and it involved a very precious man named Brother Hawley, who happened to be a missionary from the Philippines. He had a mission compound on the island of Luzon, where he was raising food, holding meetings, etc. He was speaking in a Church in Brighton, Michigan, and we felt really led to go. His message was powerful, and he really had a tremendous love and a burden for the people in the Philippines. As he spoke, I felt such a call in my heart for the Philippines, and Brother Hawley's love for the people was transferred off to me.

Brother Hawley was asking for help in his compound. He was putting together a call to pastors and wives, or to whoever felt a call, to come and help him for 10 days. I asked Dean what he felt, and he had the same burden that I had, so we went to the front after the meeting and told Brother Hawley how we felt. He was greatly encouraged by our response. He told us when it would be, and he informed us that a few others had felt the call as well. We went home with a very full heart from the meeting, and we proceeded to wait on God for the details and the money.

We shared our burden with our small Church, and they picked up the vision and the burden as well. Many people started to hand us money to save for our trip. We had a man and wife in the group at that time, and he spoke up in one of the meetings. He said that, when it came time to have all of the money and we were short, he would donate the rest. We were greatly encouraged by that.

We began to get down to the last days of gathering of the finance, for it had to be turned in very shortly. Meanwhile, the man did not come forth to give us the money. I didn't know what to do, but I finally felt to call him and see if he still was going to do what he had promised. I said "Hello," and after some small talk, I reminded him that the time was up for the finance, and we needed $300.00 to make up the difference. I reminded him of what he had said in front of the whole Church some time before. Let me say that I learned a great deal about human nature that day. He said, "No, I never promised you such a thing, and where did you ever get that idea?" Needless to say, I was totally *shocked* that someone, who had promised their help, had no intention of doing what he had offered. No one had coerced him into doing or saying anything, for it was his own decision to make the promise.

I was extremely disappointed and shocked, and I couldn't believe that he would *do* such a thing. Besides, I was frustrated in the fact that we had put down money on a ticket and would now possibly lose the money we had invested. On top of that, we still had the burden and the call on us for the Philippines.

We went to prayer about it, and the Lord laid it on my heart to go ask my father for the money. I didn't want to in any way, shape, or form to do that.

But God would not let me alone, and so I obeyed. I went to my parents' home, explained the situation, and asked if my dad would take up the slack from the other man. My father said that he knew all along that the other man would not do what he had promised. My father, then, very graciously gave us the money that we needed to pay for our fare. I thank God for such a father in my life. He was so quiet, but so precious to both Dean and me. And so, we prepared to leave for the Philippines.

We landed in Manila on a very hot day. Of course, when is it ever *cold* there? We had a very long ride to reach the mission compound. There was a total of 7 that made the trip. We were loaded into some very poor-looking taxis, along with all the luggage. We proceeded to make the long trip to our home base, where we would be staying for the next 10 days. On the way, I remember the little taxi drivers stopping at some creeks to fill their radiators with water. We never felt that we were in very trustworthy autos, but we made it.

When we reached the compound, it was time for dinner, and we were very hungry by this time. The flight over the ocean had been about 13 hours long, and so we had all been up for a very long time. There were some little Philippine servants who made our meal and cleaned up afterward. Mr. Hawley was married and had two sons. The boys were good children and obedient to their father. All the time that we were there, they were a real blessing to all of us.

Brother Hawley's wife was very strong-willed and unhappy living there: She did not share her husband's burden or vision for the people or for the island. It was a heavy load for our brother to bear, for his wife seemed to be just enduring and not enjoying the work there. She used the only fan in the house, and her attitude was very poor towards us and towards her help. Her temper was short, and it was obvious that we were a *burden* to her instead of a *blessing*. For that, we all felt sorry for her.

4c: Be Sure You Are Called

We proceeded to travel and speak in many places. It was very interesting, and we felt the love of the people in a great way. We were a group of 3 pastors, their wives, and one single lady. She had come along with one of the pastor and his wife, and it was obvious that it was not a missionary journey for her: When we would get to town of any size, she could not pass a window without primping with her hair or makeup. Yes, she wore makeup in that heat. None of the rest of us did, for all it did was to melt and streak in the heat. Perspiration was always part of every day.

We preached, prayed, and baptized the little sweet people everywhere. We were very fulfilled in all we did.

Small lizards seemed to be *everywhere* in the Philippines, and we got used to them on the ceiling, on the walls, on the walkways, and on vegetation. It was all just part of the scenery, and we got used to them after a while. One night, a pastor's wife was getting ready for bed, as well as all the rest of us. All of a sudden, we heard this piercing scream. We could hear everything anyway, for the walls never went to the ceiling so that air could move more freely in the house. Anyway, the scream was because a lizard had dropped from the ceiling and had fallen into the woman's suitcase. From the scream, it sounded much more terrible than it was. Ordinarily, the lizards were more afraid of *us* than we were of *them*. They didn't bite, and they were not vicious in any way. I don't believe the woman ever returned to the islands: She did not enjoy the trip at all.

One highlight of the trip was a communion service that we attended. Brother Hawley led us in it, and it was a communion like none that we ever had before. We have since, used it many times, and it never fails to bless everyone involved in it.

After a service, 35-70 people gathered in a very large room. Brother Hawley uncovered a full unsliced loaf of bread, and he told us that the body of Christ is all one, but consisting of many pieces. He instructed us to break off a piece of the bread and wait for the leading of the Spirit. Then, guided by the Spirit, each of us went to a particular person in the room whom the Lord had chosen, and we fed the piece of the bread to that person. We, then, hugged that person and gave him (or her) the word that the

107

Lord had given us. All I can say is "Wow!" There was such a powerful move of God in that room. We witnessed so many prophetic words and tears; it was overwhelming.

I am so grateful to Brother Hawley for teaching us to take communion that way. It says in 1 cor. 11, "When you come together, tarry for one another." It does not say, "Grab, gulp, and run." We were told that, if we felt to feed more than one person, we must be obedient. Many of us did. It was in that communion service that the one pastor's wife came to me. She fed me the bread, took me in her arms, and began to weep over me. After quite a long time, she said, "I would not be in your shoes for nothing." Little did I know what she meant that night, but I found out later that she was seeing the very thorny path that Dean and I would have to take in the days to come.

To this day, we always hold our communion services in the same manner. They never fail to bless, strengthen, encourage, and guide and lift us. If you ever do feel led to use this type of communion, leave enough time so that no one is in a hurry. We have used individual cups for the juice or a common cup, turning and wiping after each person. You will never be sorry for trying it. It will be a huge blessing.

We went into Manila the night before our flight home and stayed in a hotel near the airport. We slept in good beds and ate good food. The food in the compound was not bad, but the food in the hotel catered more to the Americans. One of the ministers had taken quite ill while we were on the island, and he was really having hard time breathing. It was almost like a pneumonia that he had contracted, and his wife was very concerned, as he was the oldest member of the team. He was a good man and did not complain, but it was obvious, to all of us, that he was not at all well.

Our flight took us to California, where we were to catch our connection to Detroit, Michigan. We missed our flight, and it meant a 6-hour layover in California. I remember the brother that was ill, trying his best to get comfortable enough to sleep in the seats without much success. We were all greatly relieved when our plane arrived and our connection was made. On the plane, we all got some short naps, but nothing that helped very much or made us feel much better. We were more relieved when the plane landed so that we could all go our separate ways. We never lost our burden for the Philippines pastors or the love for the country. We came home and shared our trip with its vision and its burden.

After our return, the Philippine people asked many times for Bibles, and we began to collect them for our next trip, for we knew that there would be a next time for us.

We ended up making about 5 long trips of ministry into the Philippines in the following years. Many of these trips included others that we were training in the ministry, and with their saying that they were genuinely called by God to go, we paid for many of their trips. We saw many wonderful things happen: Many were saved or delivered of demons; we saw some tremendous healings; and we were privileged to baptize many in the China Sea. We were asked to teach in more than one Bible school; and for many days, we stayed among the beautiful Philippine students, and we loved and taught them continually. Many pastors whom we met begged us many times to return. We had a great anointing in that country, and we never were without many, many meetings to preach in. We are grateful to God for the lessons that we learned in that country.

Chapter 5: God Moves Us on Again

5a: Move Into Town

We became restless in our wonderful home. Our two older children had moved out, and we were down to only one at home. We lived outside the city, and I kept hearing that we needed to move into town to be near more people. Dean had been feeling the same way, and so we began to move in the direction of selling our home.

The Holy Spirit had been dealing with us to get out of debt as well. We sold our travel trailer and paid off some of our debts.

Someone just came to our door one day and asked if we were selling our travel trailer, and I said that we surely were, even though we had no sign on it, etc. They bought it on the spot with cash. Then, God led us to cash in our insurance policies, and with that, we paid off some more things. He spoke to us that, through the sale of our home, we would buy another place and pay cash for it. We, then, would be truly out of debt.

The sale of the house was very quick. In three weeks or so, it sold. The people that bought it were good solid people, and they had no problem getting a loan. The value of the home had gone up considerably during our 14 years in it, so we cleared over $35,000 on it. That would have been in 1977. We had the hugest garage sale in history and moved in December of '77.

We began to look for our new home, as we only had a short time to get out of our old one. We enlisted the same realtor as the one who had sold the old home. He ran himself ragged searching for a place for us. God had said that our next home would be paid in full, so we could not look at homes for more than what we had cleared. The realtor continued to take us to homes where we would have to carry a small mortgage, and we kept telling him "No." We could not look at things over our price. He was so frustrated with us, but we knew that we had to obey what we had heard.

One day, I was vacuuming the floor, and I heard God say, "It is not on the market yet." The realtor called soon after that, and I told him that it was not on the market yet. When he asked me again to see a more expensive home, he said, "How do you know that?" I told him that *God* had given me the

115

information. Needless to say, he was very surprised by my answer. It wasn't very long after that when I received a call again from him, asking me to drive past a home that had just been listed. It was in an older section of the city, but he thought that it might meet our needs.

I drove by the home in the afternoon, and it looked quite good from the outside. It had a small fenced yard and a rather run-down garage, but the home had aluminum siding and decent windows, and the roof looked good. I went back home and called the realtor and set up an appointment to go through the home that very day. When Dean came home from work, we went to see it, and when we walked in, we took one look around and said, "How much did you say this house was?" He looked at the listing and said, "Surely this price is wrong, for it is only $27,000 dollars." We were all pleasantly *surprised* to say the least.

The home had plastered walls with coved ceilings, and the floors were carpeted. There were 3 bedrooms, a bath, a kitchen with a small eating area, a dining room, living room, full finished basement, small workshop, laundry area, and storage shelves. On the end of the large recreation room was a partitioned-off room, which had beautiful built-in shelves and a place for desks for study. There was a flight of stairs with a door off the dining room that went up to the second floor. The area up there was all unfinished, but it had the subfloor, and it would not take much work to finish it. We knew right away that this was our place, so we offered $25,000, and the owners accepted it. They had another place to go to. So, with us with cash and them ready to move on, it was without complication that the move was made.

We moved in two weeks before Christmas in 1977. There were a number of things that we wanted to do with our new home. I painted all the way through to start with, and we put down new floors in the stairway to the basement and in the kitchen. Then we had the carpets cleaned and hung new drapes throughout -- what a difference it made.

The tenants before us were career people, and the home needed some TLC. We purchased a beautiful dining room set, and it felt so good and right. We, then, bought a ping-pong table and a pool table for the basement, for we used our basement for the youth of our Church, and they held their meetings there. The whole setup was so perfect for our needs at that time. There was the cutest ceramic fireplace in the basement, and we loved it. We would build a fire and just enjoy the whole area. We loved our new little home, and we were very happy doing what we were doing. I remember so well getting up at night and walking through our home and saying, "We really own this house." It seemed such an awesome thing to have a home paid off. We were praising God for taking us out of debt. The home was inexpensive to heat and light, and the taxes were small, for it was in an older part of town. Dean was still working at his regular job; so, for the first time in our lives, we were better off than we had ever been.

5b: Connie Hears Another Call

I was very happy in our new home, and one day, I was vacuuming in the basement and just praising the Lord when I heard his voice say, "I want you to be ordained." I stopped my work and said, "What? . . . Why must I be ordained?" He said, "I want you to be ordained." Well, Dean's folks were very staunch Baptists, and they did not believe in women in the ministry. I wondered how our own children would accept it, and I really did not want to have that kind of attention in my life, so I resisted his call. I never told a soul what I heard that day in the basement, but the Spirit of God would not leave me alone.

I answered the phone one day, and while I was speaking to the individual on the line, God said to me, "This is why I want you ordained." I had begun to counsel with people a good deal, and that is what he meant. People love papers and titles, and even though they meant nothing to Dean and me, God had a greater plan that we did not know about: We would be traveling everywhere in the future, and we needed to have that paper for those who could not recognize the call of God on a life without it. So reluctantly, I finally said to Dean, "What would you say if I told you that I am supposed to be ordained?" I have the best husband in the world: He said, "Then you better do it."

It did not take long after that to get an ordination service together. Dean's parents did not attend, even though they were invited. We respected their stand: They believed in what their truth was in the matter, and they stood in it. We had to stand in our truth as well. We had a great service. It was highly anointed and many prophecies came, and with the elders of our little group, God set me into his work.

The little Church was doing well. The people were growing and we were all learning a lot. We were learning, in particular, about trusting God and letting him have his way in every service. With Dean's job with Western Electric, he had to go on transfer away from home at times. There would be new offices to install equipment in, and when he finished in one location, they would send him off to another. Sometimes they were close enough to drive to, but many times, he would have to be gone for long periods of time, even *months* before he could get home.

Dean received a notice from his company at this time. They were sending him to Indiana, and that would mean that he would be gone for long periods of time. He had 25 years in with his company, and he knew in his heart, that he had come to a "Y" in the road. He would have to make a decision: Would he go full-time as a minister and retire from the other job, or would he keep the other job and leave the Church to Ben and me to run it. We were both coming forth in our ministries very well, but we knew at that time, that *Dean* was the one called. After much prayer on his own, we prayed together on our knees one night. Our prayer concerned whether to work another 5 years and have our Blue Cross - Blue Shield paid for the rest of our lives, or was God saying, "Leave it all." After praying one night, Dean had a message in tongues, and God gave me the interpretation. God said, "Don't worry about insurance, for *I* am your insurance."

We went before the people and asked if they could see their way clear enough to giving us $100.00 per week for a wage and help with some of the home's expenses. If they could, Dean would retire from Western Electric and go full-time in ministry. They said that they were well able to do that for us, and so with that commitment, Dean retired, and we lost all of our benefits. He had earned a small pension, which he began to collect right away.

Chapter 6: A New Life

6a: The Challenge to Greater Giving

A new life of faith on our part had begun. We still had a teen-age son at home eating as only a teen can eat, and it was a real financial challenge. When that happened, we heard God say, "Give me 20 percent now." We had always been tithers, but now, out of the $100.00 per week, we had to put $20.00 in the plate. That left only $80.00, and that did not go far even in 1978. We had some real struggles with our faith, but we would remind each other what God's word said, and we would rise above it once more.

Our youngest son Danny was getting ready for graduation from high school, and one day, he came home and informed us that he was going to join the Marine Corps. He wondered what our reaction would be to this news. Dean told him that if *he* (Dean) had chosen, he would not have chosen the marines, but he said, "You have to live your life." As for me, I, of course, told him that my mother's (i.e., *Connie's*) heart was not real thrilled with his decision, but I likewise said, "You must live your own life."

We gave him an open house as we had with our other two children, and the following weekend after graduation, he got on a bus to leave home for the first time in his life. He was 19 years old and had never even spent a night with any of his friends before. He always was a very soft, tender-spirited child, and off he went to the hardest part of the service in our land. Of course, I felt very sad, but God helps us with *everything* if we let him. I had been very emotional at the graduation exercises, and I had been led, at that time, to get out his baby book and all the pictures that we had taken of his years growing up, and I relived every memory. Then, I heard God say, "Now close the book and release him." I did that night, and when he (Danny) left, I wept, but not as much as I had on his graduation. So he was off on his own adventure.

He had some problems adjusting to such a different kind of mind-set. The physical end of training was very difficult as well. Danny was like the rest of us, always a bit overweight. They put him on what is called the "Fat Farm," and they watched every mouthful he ate. He ended up breaking a foot, and that set him back in the training time.

He had been in for about 6 weeks when we received our first call from him. He had only 5 minutes to speak, and his first sentence was, "Mom, I can't believe people *treat* people like this." Then he would cry, he would utter another sentence, and he would cry again. He was so emotionally upset over being called every name in the book and being treated like so much garbage. I know they say that they have to "*break* them to *make* them," but he was always such a soft-hearted child that this was extremely difficult for him. He made it though, and on the first trip home, I couldn't believe the difference in him: He was so slim and so muscular; we had never seen him like that in all of his life. His eyes were very dark underneath, and I could sense the suffering that he had experienced to gain the marine status. He ended up making a career of it for

20 years, but he had a lot of rough moments getting there.

We had work to do for the Lord, and so we headed into our next adventure. I was led to do some volunteer work at a school to help students to read, and I did that for a number of months. At this time, I had been active in the women's "Aglow," an organization for women where we would come together and eat, listen to a speaker, and engage in personal ministry. It was a good group, and in the beginning, I was asked to be a counselor; and later, I was asked to *lead* the counselors.

During one of the meetings, I sat beside a minister's wife from London, Ontario, Canada. We had a wonderful talk, and the others sitting around us were very interested in what we were talking about. Our topic was on inner healing, i.e., healing of the memories. I have always been very intuitive, often knowing many things without any input, just the voice of God inside of me. I have also always been interested in the mind and how it works. I had done some reading on the topic and had shared what I knew about it. In any event, the lady asked me if I would be interested in coming to their United Church on a Saturday and teach a seminar. Little did she know that I had told her all that I knew in a matter of a few minutes, and I sure did not know what I would say for a whole day. I heard myself say, "Yes, I could do that." Of course, I was hoping, at the time, that it would never come to pass. We continued with the meeting; we exchanged names, addresses, and phone numbers; and I thought, "So much for that."

Soon after, I was led to do a 10-day fast. One day, as I was breaking my fast, Dean went to the mailbox. He took out a letter from the mailbox and noticed that it was addressed to me, and as he entered the house, he said, "Here is an invitation for you to speak." I said, "No, it is not," and he said, "Yes, it is, for I just heard God tell me that." I opened the letter, and it was that same minister's wife, with an invitation to come on a certain date at a certain time at their Church in London, Ontario to hold a seminar on inner healing. I was overwhelmed, surprised, shocked, and scared. I felt inadequate, unprepared, and so lacking in the knowledge necessary for this task. God told me that I would go. During this time, we had been praying over people for inner healing, and we saw God do many wonderful healings right in our own home.

I went immediately to the bookstore and bought every book that I could find on inner healing or healing of the memories. I began to study everything that I could put my hands on about the topic. I was diligent in prayer, and of course, I called the lady and said, "Yes, I can do that for you." We laid the plans thinking that there would be only 10-15 women, but little did we know what was to come.

Dean drove me there, and because it was a woman's meeting, he had to spend the day somewhere else. I went in with my seminar notes and met the minister's wife, and she informed me that it had grown much larger than what she had expected. We ended up with approximately 40-50 women. That in itself brought me to my knees in prayer. The Lord was so marvelous to me. I spoke for an hour or so. Then we had a small break before I spoke for another hour or so. I led them in a group meditation of inner healing, and I don't remember a word of what I said to this day. It wasn't me anyway; it was all God. There were many tears all over the room, and much healing went on that only the Spirit of God knows about. Afterward, they asked me if they could speak to me one-on-one, and I said "Yes." I had very little to eat, for the need was so great. One by one, they came into a room that I had been given the use of, and one by one, they went out smiling with tears running down their faces. Dean had returned to the Church and was watching them come out crying and smiling all at the same time. He was thinking that it must have been a good meeting, and he was right. Someone told him to come in and eat something, so he did. When the last woman left the counseling room, I was exhausted, but I was so very happy at what God did with a simple farm girl who said "Yes" to him. He had truly given me a special anointing for that day and for the needs of the women. We drove home praising God.

Out of that meeting, we began to be asked to teach once a week in Ailsa Craig, Ontario and in some of the other small towns in that area. We went to one dear sister's place for quite a length of time. They loved the word I would bring by the Spirit, and we always had a lunch and good fellowship afterward. About this time, I had been searching and hungry for the truth of God's word, and one day, he showed me that there was not the kind of "Rapture" that we had studied much of our lives. I was told that every time I received another revelation of the deeper things of God, I was being Raptured. That is an experience that I have had over and over, and I praise him for that! I knew that it was the truth, for it rang in my spirit so strong. I got up to minister the word the following week, and out of my mouth came the very words that I had determined I would not say. The Spirit had a different idea, and needless to say, that was our last time there. They did not want their old ideas challenged, and so that door closed. They had the minister of the United Church where I had held the seminar speak from then on. I know they thought that I was just too radical for them. We accepted it as the Will of God and did not explain away what we had said. We moved on.

6b: God's Insurance Comes Through

One evening, Dean began to experience chest pains and a radiating pain down his arm. We had no insurance, but I insisted that we go to the emergency room for help. Dean said, "Absolutely not!" We prayed and stayed home, for *God* was our insurance; God had *promised* that to us. I was very concerned, and my mind went *everywhere* as far as my fear about his health. I asked him over and over to let me take him to the hospital, and over and over he said "No." He agonized in pain all night, and neither of us slept much. When morning came, he looked really haggard from the pain and the lack of rest. He sat around with no energy all day, and I kept asking him if he would go, and I finally gave up. I never gave up praying, and little by little, he got a little better. I finally got him to agree to go and have an electrocardiogram. I was very worried that he might have damaged his heart.

We went to the doctor and explained that we were ministers without insurance, and the doctor said "Okay." He tested Dean, and we went to leave the office. I went to the desk and asked what we owed, and the receptionist said "Nothing"; it was free. I was so excited about what God had done that on our way out, I said, "I don't think you realize what God did back there." Dean said, "I don't think you realize what God just did here in this entrance." Dean felt God touch him and heal him in that entryway at that moment in time. Hallelujah! *God* was our insurance. There was no damage to his heart, and it is many years later. He is still wonderful. How can we ever praise our great God enough!

The demand for us to travel and speak began to pick up. More calls came in, and our hearts were beginning to be stirred for the nations of this world. We knew that change was coming again. Our congregation had grown some, and we were very happy and growing in the Lord.

Our oldest son Benny, and his wife, were such a support to us at that time. They had birthed our first grandchild by this time. His name was Aaron, and he was born on September 5, 1978. They didn't live too far from us at that time, and so they came over often. We loved our grandson, and of course, he was the most beautiful child ever created. We enjoyed many happy hours with Benny and his family.

Our basement was finished, and we had toys down there for Aaron. He could toddle all over very early, and we would watch him enjoy the freedom of the large area. He was so busy learning so much as they all do. One evening, Benny and his family were visiting us. Aaron went to run across the floor, and I said, "Aaron, you come to Grandma, Grandma loves you so very much." I heard the voice of God say, "You love him too much." Little did I know what was coming down the road.

Dean and I began to be stirred in our spirit to travel and teach. We had been praying as to what the Lord wanted for us, and after seeking the Lord for some time, we felt that we saw the plan. We would convert the unfinished attic into a small apartment for Dean and me. Then, our son Benny, his wife

Janet, and their son Aaron would move into the lower floor of the house. Benny would leave his job and live on the small money that the Church would pay him. We, then, would be free to go out and move as the Lord would lead us. We would remain on the board of the Church as senior ministers, and Benny would become the main minister for all the meetings. The people really loved Benny and his family a lot, and they accepted this arrangement as the will of the Lord.

We all began to build our new little place upstairs, and it came together so nicely and so quickly. On one end of the upstairs was a small kitchen, which contained an apartment-size refrigerator and stove, a small cupboard, a very tiny table, and two chairs. On the other end was a very large bedroom and sitting area. There was an area by the stairway that served as a closet, and in the middle, we built a full bath. We installed a small stainless steel sink to wash dishes, as well as for our cleansing. We had a nice shower, and it was all we needed, as we were *gone* so much of the time. For some time, we had been traveling up to London, Ontario, Canada, about 70 miles east of us; we went up twice a week. The home that was open for us was in the low-income projects there, and we stayed in the home of a lovely woman that was very hungry for the deeper things of God. She gave up her bed many times for us, as we often would go the night before the meeting so that we wouldn't have to travel so early in the morning. It was a small group, about 10-12 people, but we had some powerful meetings.

We made a smooth transition of our going out and our son moving into our home and into the work of God full time. It was really a pleasure to have them in our home. We respected their privacy, and they did ours. Many mornings, we would call down and ask Aaron to come up. We would make toast and cook him an egg, and he would enjoy that so much. We really felt that we had the best life that anyone could have. God was so real, the word was awesome, the people hungry, our family was close, and we were very content.

Chapter 7: European Adventures

7a: The Call to Europe

On June 22, 1980, we were in a Sunday morning meeting in London, Ontario. I was ministering the word, and all of a sudden, the Spirit of God swept into the room like a wave. We all began to weep, and I knew I had to wait on the Lord. We stood still, praised the Lord, and cried. Then, I heard the Lord say that, if everyone would get on their knees and wait on him, he would speak to everyone in the room. We obeyed, and as I waited, I heard the word "Germany." I knew that we did not know anyone in Germany, and we sure could not *speak* the language. After a short amount of time, we all got up, and when we had all calmed down from the weeping, I said, "If anyone would like to share what they had received, please do so." One by one, they began to share what they had heard. Dean and I didn't share what *we* had heard, for neither of us understood what in the world was going on. I proceeded to preach the word, and as usual, Dean duplicated the tapes for those who had requested them.

We were fellowshipping around the table afterward when Dean began to exhort a brother across the table. He said, "What does it matter if God told you to quit your job and go to Germany?" I was shocked! I said to him, "Why did you say *Germany*?" He replied, "Because that is what I heard when I knelt today." I knew, then, there was a plan in the Spirit that we had only seen a small part of on that particular day, but God was faithful to unfold the fullness of the plan as we kept saying "Yes" and moving forward!

At that time, we had plans to attend the End Time Handmaidens Convention that was coming up on July 1, in St. Louis, Missouri. While there, one day, the presence of the Lord came into the meeting, much like he had done in Canada for us. Sister Gwen Shaw was ministering, and she exhorted us to get on our knees and wait on the Lord for his direction. We fell to our knees, Dean on one chair and me on another, and many others around us did the same. There was a lot of weeping, and it was a wonderful time of a visitation of God's presence. As I wept, I heard in my spirit, "You will go to Berlin, Germany, and you will go August 10. I was truly surprised, as that was not very long to wait. I was also told that we would go for forty days. When the

Spirit's presence lifted, I said to Dean, "Did you receive anything?" He said, "No, did *you*?" I said "Yes" and then gave him what I heard. Dean said, "It looks like it won't be long then."

We came home and began to get into the word. We were instructed to fast for 21 days to prepare ourselves for what was coming. One morning in prayer and Bible-reading, the Lord gave me Numbers 11:23, "And the Lord said unto Moses, 'Is the Lord's hand waxed short? Thou shalt see now whether my word shall come to pass unto thee or not.'" On another day, he gave numbers 13:25, "And they returned from searching the land after forty days." With every Scripture, we were more and more assured that we had heard rightly. On another morning, I received Deuteronomy 1:21, "Behold, the Lord thy God hath set the land before thee, go up and possess it, as the Lord God of thy fathers hath said unto thee; fear not, neither be discouraged." What a blessing every promise was to us. What an encouragement to keep us believing in our God. Another day, I received Deuteronomy 6:23, "And he brought us out from thence, that he might bring us in, to give us the land which he swear unto our fathers." And also Deuteronomy 31:8, "And the Lord, he it is that doth go before thee; he will be with thee, he will not fail thee, neither forsake thee, fear not, neither be dismayed." So much comfort, day-by-day, as we fasted and waited.

7b: The cost

And then came the friends in the Lord. Do you have friends in the Lord? We all do, but some don't give much support when you are called to a very different kind of call. We heard everything from, "How can you afford it?" to "How can you do that?" to "How good is your hearing? Thank God that we had the Scriptures that he had given, but most of all, we had heard a direct living word to our spirits. It is called "Rhema," a living word, personal, direct, "no doubt" kind of word, and that is what held us.

We had to buy our tickets 3 weeks ahead to lock in the lowest price. We opened the map of Germany, laid our hands on Berlin, and began to weep and travail for the people there. God let us feel their cry and their burden for help in gaining some strength for their difficult walk.

The next day, we went to the travel service to purchase our tickets. When we got there, no seats were available for our flight on August 10. We didn't panic; we stood and said, "That is when we have to go." The girl kept looking. All of a sudden, she said, "Oh! Wait a minute. I see 2 available seats on that flight." Yes, we knew that there *had* to be 2 available seats: The Lord had spoken, and they were *ours*. We had collected enough for one ticket, and we had to charge the other, but it was paid off quickly later on.

We had a number of groups that we were ministering to at that time, and one day, in one of the groups, a lady stood up and began to prophesy over us that the ministry in Germany would be glorious. Many others, that day, brought words over us also. One sister saw us before a gate, and the word "Shalom" was over it. We did not understand *then*, but later in Vienna, Austria, in the mission house that we worked out of, there was a sign on the wall that read "Shalom"; God spoke to me and said, "This is the gate that was seen." Vienna was the gateway to all of Eastern Europe, and most missions worked out of Vienna.

Let me say here that, when the lady prophesied that the ministry would be glorious, we get some kind of an image about these things. "Glorious" to God is truly death to the flesh, as that is the glorious part.

I would like to say as well that the word "minister" means to *serve*; it does not mean to *preach*. To serve means that you are willing to roll up your sleeves, clean toilets, wash floors, weed gardens, make meals, etc. Many want titles that keep them from getting involved physically with the "work" of the Lord, but it all is necessary, and above all, we need a servant's heart to really be like our master Jesus Christ.

After we bought our tickets, a supernatural peace descended on us. We were told by the Lord that he would be there in Berlin, Germany, waiting for us when we got off the plane: He was true to his word.

We went to the Church that God had used us to begin, and we stood up and shared our news, expecting the people to feel as *we* did. We were a little confused, but excited about where it would take us. Unfortunately, the people didn't support us, not even our own son and his wife, who were *living* with us. We were so naïve at this time and did not realize just how it had upset them. We continued to pray and fast, and that is what really let all hell break loose in our lives.

We didn't have any idea as to what we would do or where we would stay yet. We kept praying, fasting, traveling, speaking, and sharing our news about the trip to Germany. Little by little the money began to come in for our trip. We never begged for anything, for we are not beggars; we are the king's children, and he is more than enough.

I was sitting at my desk one day, and above it on the wall, we had hung a map of the world. As I studied, prayed, and talked to God, I heard the cries of the people calling out for help. For just a moment in time, the Holy Spirit let me hear and feel just what God must feel when so many need so much all the time. I sat and wept with the burden that I was feeling for the world.

Some days later, the phone rang, and it was the president of the women's Aglow Group where I led the counselors. I had shared with them about our call to Germany earlier. She had a burden for us as to our having no phone numbers to contact when we got there, and so she gave me the number of the leader of all the women's Aglow in Europe. She felt that she was told by God to do that, for it may be that the leader of the women's Aglow in Europe would be the channel that God would work through to connect us to the people we needed to help. I thanked her and assured her that we were not worrying about how it would all happen. We would be very grateful for the woman's number later, but at that moment, we did not know just how important it would be.

God had spoken to us: We would have $1,000.00 to go on this journey. Then he began to challenge us to give out certain amounts to different people. Of course, the natural mind says, "How will I have enough if I give?" The principal of God is, "Give, and you shall receive." So we obeyed. We always were living by God's principals, not always understanding them fully, but doing what we knew to do. The money continued to come in, and we continued to set it aside.

In the meantime, our son and his wife were growing very angry over this whole trip. I remember coming home from teaching somewhere and opening the back door, and I could actually feel the pressure of hands on my chest pushing me out the door. God showed me that it was their thoughts forming the pressure that was against the whole walk that Dean and I were making at that time. They were responding in fear, pride, and some control-factors as well. Thoughts are *things*; they really are, and they have *power*. We loved them so very much, and we still do. It was a very difficult time for all of us. We did not blame anyone *then*, and we do not blame anyone *now*. It was as it was, but it was a tremendous test for us, and we passed it.

We found out later that there were some, in the small Church where Benny pastored for us, who had built up his ego: They said that he was so much greater than Dean and I in the category of ministering the word. Our children separated themselves from us; they wouldn't speak to us anymore; and there was certainly no more fellowship in our home. It became a place where we were all very uncomfortable. In all our lives, it was the darkest, hardest thing that we had ever walked through. Our other children became confused by it, as they did not know just what to believe.

We had gone somewhere to speak, and when we came home, we went to one of the member's home to speak with them. When we got there, we were told that they had gone to a board meeting in someone's home. Dean and I were still on the board as the senior pastors, and we were not told about the meeting. We were told by God to go to the meeting, so we did. When we walked in, they were all very surprised. We were the last ones they wanted to see. We asked why we had not been included, and we were told that they were having the meeting to vote us off the board because of our going to Germany. They felt that we needed to go back to the Philippines instead, as very often, we had received many letters begging us to come back. We had Bibles stacked up to take there, and we could understand their confusion. The problem was that there was no call spiritually to the Philippines; the call in the Spirit was to *Germany*.

God is the leader and we are the followers, and we knew that we had heard the voice of God's Spirit say *Germany*. We could not go to the Philippines instead. It mattered not that the Church no longer wanted us or our children were miserable about it; we had to obey. Our lives have always been different, and we are aware of it. We didn't understand the call ourselves, so how could we expect *others* to understand it. God does not ask us to understand, but just to do what he says. It was

155

one of the most painful things that Dean and I have ever walked through in our lives. After being so close to our children, and now to be cut away, it was heartbreaking. We could not comply with their wishes to make everyone happy, for then, the great God that we know would not be pleased. It is better to have our *family* unhappy than to make our *Father* unhappy. It was a very lonely time for us, for we were not allowed to be near our grandchildren anymore.

By now, Ben and Janet had had their second son Danny. I remember coming in the house one day, and Janet was seated and feeding the baby. I reached out to touch the baby's head, and she told me not to touch him. I knew that she was really upset, and I honored her request from then on. It was more than a difficult time for all of us. It was a very necessary thing though, as we had to completely and fully give ourselves to the European work. It took our all, and we could not be worrying about the family back home while on duty there. We love our children so very much, and our relationship has been healed as much as it can be. We are all much older and wiser, and we release each other to make our own walk. That time was a great time to depend on the grace of God to get us all through.

Finally, on August 10 of 1980, it was time to head for the airport. We were promised by the Spirit to have a thousand dollars to go, but we were short by $50.00 when we left for the airport. My parents and a friend drove us down and dropped us off. We said our goodbyes, and my parents promised to pray for us every day, which I know they did. It was what gave us strength and courage to do the job we were sent to do. Just as we were getting ready to board and disappear into the plane, a little pastor that we had met and helped financially came running and waving a bill. He said, "Pastor Smith, Pastor Smith." Just as we could wait no longer, the last $50.00 came in, just as God had said. What a great God we serve!

It was an overnight flight, letting us land in the morning in Frankfort, where we had about an hour's layover to connect with the plane that would deliver us to our destination. A very precious brother and sister in the Lord met us in Frankfort, and we had a time of fellowship with them. They encouraged us to stop there, go out and preach with them around the area, and then after our 40 days, go home from there. We thanked them for the invitation, but we knew when we sat in that airport that we were not where the Lord had said. If we would have sold out to the flesh and stayed, we would have had it easy. We would have had a nice place to sleep, good food to eat, and many appreciating us and loving us for the word that we would bring. However, it was not the perfect will of God, and so we said thank-you, but no, thank-you. We blessed the couple and boarded the plane to the true destination.

Oh, the mixture of thoughts we had as we waited for the flight to end. We didn't sleep much, and we were in jetlag when we landed. As we disembarked from the plane, we looked up, and there in a vision very clearly, the image of the Christ was already there with his arms open, saying, "You have come to the right place, welcome to Berlin." What an overwhelming feeling of comfort and assurance that we received from that confirming sign that day. He is so good, and he knew that we needed to be encouraged. It was a huge thing to get in a plane with no information about where we would go, what we would do, and have only one phone number on us. God had called us and we had answered, and that was all that we were sure of right then. There certainly was some fear in both of us, and yet a tremendous peace as well.

One day before we had left America, I was in prayer, and I was feeling a great deal of fear as I prayed. I confessed to God my fear, and I felt that I was failing him and his call. I begged him to forgive my fear and give me courage. He said this to me, "Connie, great love gives great courage." What a precious lesson I learned that day, and I held on to it throughout all of our trips. I said on that day, "Yes, Lord, and I love you so much. I will have great courage for you."

We got our luggage, and we had packed too much, of course. We brought a lot of good clothes, as we thought we might be preaching a lot, etc. When we arrived, we walked around in the airport trying to get our bearings as to the fact that we were really here now. Then, Dean said to me, "Why don't you call that number; what do we have to lose?"

Have you ever made a call in a foreign country to someone you never met and say, "God sent me."? Well, I did: I explained to this lady that her number had been given to me by the president of women's Aglow in Sarnia, Ontario, Canada, as she thought that I might be needing some help in the Aglow here in Europe. I said, "I hope you don't think I am crazy, but all I am telling you is true of our call and our journey here." The woman was wonderful to us. She said, "I don't think you are crazy at all, because I witness with your spirit." She didn't know just what part she would play in our stay there, but she proceeded to tell us that she had just gotten back from a long journey to all the Aglows herself, and she wouldn't have been there if we had come a day earlier. God's timing is so perfect, *always*. She told us to go and find a pension (similar to hotels or motels in the United States.) and get some rest. In the meantime, she would pray and we would pray, to see just what God's plan would be for us while we were there. We were to call her the next day, and we would compare notes as to what we had received in prayer.

We looked in the airport for information on where to stay. We needed a place where they could speak English, for we could not understand German. So we asked at the desk and were directed to another area where, for a fee, they would hook us up with a pension that had workers who could speak English. We paid the fee and they made the call, and we proceeded to get directions for the bus that would take us to the pension. What a time we had. We found the right bus, but we did not understand where to get off. Fortunately, a Mennonite man on the bus spoke English, and he asked us if we were new to the area. We explained that we had just arrived, and he told us where our stop was; and he helped us to unload our luggage. He was truly a blessing to us; he was one of God's many angels along our way.

We had to carry so much weight for such a long walk, and we were very weary by now. We came to the pension where the airport had sent us, and a lady up on the second floor asked if we were the "Smith" party. We answered "Yes," and she directed us into the house. She showed us our room and the bath that we would be using, and we proceeded to get settled in and make some cup-of-soup and some instant coffee to fill up the emptiness within. We had bought the necessary equipment to do this, and we were very glad we did. The coffee on the streets of Berlin was $1.75 per cup, and our $1000.00 would not last very long at that rate.

We proceeded to take a nap and get our bearings a little bit. We felt much better afterward, and so we went out to walk and feel the heartbeat of the city. Berlin is like New York or California. It is very modern, very fashionable, and in vogue so to speak. It was uncomfortable to a certain degree for Dean and me, as we are small-town folks with country roots. We saw some of the buildings that had been bombed in the Second World War that were still standing, and I remember seeing the Kaiser Wilhelm Church and what was left of it. The young people were hanging around it, and it seemed to be a drug center, for there was buying-and-selling going on, and some of them looked very high. Dean and I had a burden for their aimless empty lives, and we prayed for them, but we were not there for that.

We called the head of the women's Aglow the following afternoon after we had a good night's sleep, more walking, and more praying. She said that she still didn't know what we were there for. Then she hesitated for a moment and asked if we would go into the "East," and we said "Yes." We knew that, when she said the word "East," it meant going behind the Iron Curtain. She said that she had to make a call, and we were to call her back. There was a delay of time before we could make the call, and so we killed some more time on the streets, resting, and making more cup-of-soup, etc.

We, again, made the call to her after a period of time had gone by, and she said that she had connected us with the East Europe Mission. She gave us instructions about them, and through a series of U-bahn rides (underground railroad, etc.), we found the address. We were welcomed warmly by lovely people, where we spent a number of hours with the people of the mission. They showed us slides of the work that they were doing, which was smuggling Bibles into countries behind the Iron Curtain. They explained very thoroughly how they worked and what it involved: the special-built cars and campers, the money that the smugglers received for gas and food, the contacts' names and addresses. Then, the big question came. They looked right at us and asked, "Will you go?" We both said, "Yes, we will go." It was not *people* asking us that question; it was *God himself* testing our willingness to do what he had sent us for.

7c: The Work Begins

Immediately, the plans were laid to go to the pension where we were staying, pick up our clothes, etc., and get us settled in the mission house. The mission was located just 5 blocks from the "wall" that separated East and West Berlin. What a great place for a mission. The darkness was very real where we stayed, for the thought processes of mankind are very real and form a sense of heaviness and bondage when they are against the light of God. We did a great deal of praying for the Communists during our stay at the mission.

Upon our arrival at the mission, we were told that we would be in charge of the place. They handed us the keys and said that everyone would be gone making trips to smuggle Bibles for the next 3-4 days, and we would be alone in the mission home. We were amazed at their trust in us. We shouldn't have been though, as when they asked us how we had come to Germany, we let them know our entire story from the call to the cost to come. They said no one had ever come to them that way before, for usually people learned of the mission and came that way. We were unique in our arrival there.

During the next few days, when Dean and I were alone in the place, we just did whatever we could to be helpful. We cleaned the place thoroughly first, and then we washed all the bedding, for many would be returning and need clean sheets and towels. Then, as I recall, there was a small garden in the back, and some of the vegetables were ready, so we brought them in and prepared them for use. Many times, we just walked the 5 blocks to the wall and watched the guards walking and looking, and we prayed for their eyes to be opened to their bondage. We prayed that our great God who loved them so very much would somehow get through the darkness that they were living in.

Many times in the night while we were there, I would wake up with such a feeling of a dark presence in the room. If I had known what I know now, it would not have been so hard. But I didn't, so I would just lie in bed and pray for many hours sometimes. After a while, the presence would lift, and I would sleep once more. It was a true school of learning for us.

For the next few days, after all the smugglers had returned from their successful trips, we just remained there listening and learning. The mission heads were trying to arrange a trip for us into East Berlin, but every time that it seemed to be set up, the pieces would fall apart. I believe that we were there waiting for about 3 days or so when the mission leader approached us and said that he could put us in a car and send us to Vienna, Austria to another branch of the East Europe mission. We agreed and got into the car with all of our luggage, and we went willingly to Austria.

They had to obtain a transit visa to make the trip. We had to cross East Berlin and some of East Germany. Now, with a transit visa, we could not stop for anything except for fuel. If they would see us on the road, we could be in serious trouble. They said "Big Brother" was watching us all the time, and Big Brother, of course, meant the Communist Government.

What a beautiful part of the world these countries are, with so many beautiful mountains, hills, and forests. God's glory was seen everywhere, but I am not sure how much we enjoyed it then, as we were really conscious of the depth of the call of God and its *seriousness* in our lives. Our minds were very intent on the work waiting for us.

We arrived in late afternoon in Austria after a 13-hour journey. It was on a Thursday. We were met by a beautiful little Swiss lady named Bella, and she was so pretty, with lovely blonde hair, blue eyes, and a petite figure that all women would envy. Her husband's name was Martin, and they were the hosts of the mission during our entire stay there. This mission was the main one; the other one in Berlin was a part-timers mission. We were asked how long we had to serve, and when we told them, they were very happy. We would not be just a quick trip in-and-out, but a possibility of many trips over the next weeks of our allotted time. Oh, how very innocent we were, when I think back, as to what we had said "Yes" to. It was very difficult on the flesh, for most of us here in America don't know what real hardship is until we are challenged, and we were. We know that we were not the only ones to ever do this work, but they really saw very few Americans who came to do such things.

They showed us to our room, and they showed us where the bathing facilities were. What a surprise that was. They were so different from here, but we adjusted quickly. We arranged our clothing, settled in, and tried to get our bearings concerning where we were as far as location went. We met others that were staying in this mission house, waiting for their orders to carry God's word to those that were in bondage. We enjoyed our times of getting to know everyone there. Most of them could speak English, for which we were grateful. We never, in all of our travels, ever had a problem with language. Everywhere God led us, we always had people that could speak and interpret for us. We never could have waited for someone, or some Church, to educate us for the work that we faced. It would have taken us the rest of our lives in preparation, and the work would never have gotten done.

In a day or two, we were asked to go and see the autos and campers that were special-built to carry the Bibles in secret compartments. We were very happy to do so. How interesting that day was, and Dean and I were amazed at the talent and anointing that was involved in the preparation of the vehicles for this very dangerous work. They were completely transformed by a little Swiss man who could look at a vehicle and see just where the compartments could be placed and where they would be least likely to be found out. What a wonderful Lord we serve, to give such a gift to someone to completely fool the enemy. God's word can never be bound, and here was our proof. Again, it was an education that we get from books.

7d: The Challenge

In a short time, late one afternoon, we were approached to make our first journey; it would be to

Romania. A man came, spread out maps in front of us, and half in German and half in very broken English, we were so-called briefed as to the trip that we would be making. We were told that we would cross the border at Jimbolia, and our mission was in Timisorara, Romania. We had to memorize the addresses of the people that we would be going to. When he finished, he asked if there were any questions, and I felt like saying, "Yes, what did you just say?" I don't know, to this day, how we ever remembered it all, but with the help of God, we did.

We were given a Toyota camper, and its floor was full of Bibles. There was a secret way to open it, and we were given the combination for its use. Dean had to do something with the ignition, and I stood on the passenger side and carried out another process. When these two things were done, an electric motor would engage, and the floor would open up like a scroll. The first time we worked it, we felt like James Bond or someone of that caliber. It had been English-built. So yes, the driver was on the right side, and what a complication that was, as the European roads were like ours here. Dean could not see anything, so I had to read maps, tell him when to cross roads, and really be his eyes for him. We were given the names of the contacts where the Bibles would be left, and we were instructed as to their handling. The names and addresses were to be kept secret, for if the government found out who were receiving the forbidden materials, they would be made to suffer a great deal.

One day, before we left, I had a vision of a man in a large room, and he was handing us $1,000.00. I told Dean what I had seen, and we had no idea how that would all come to pass. Here, on this day, it was fulfilled, for the man was talking to us all in a very large room, and then he handed us 1000 Deutsch marks, and 1000 Austrian shillings, which equaled 1000 American dollars, and so the vision was fulfilled.

We were instructed to go to the store and buy a few things to eat for the journey, for the food was very scarce behind the Iron Curtain, and they were of very poor quality. We had no idea as to how much we would need, and it was just the grace of God that we did what we did. We were truly overwhelmed with the responsibility. Usually, the mission sent us out in two sets of two, and we were placed with a Dutch couple whom we had met and learned to like very much. Their names were Jaap and Jeanette, and they had a child named Emmanuel, which means, "God is with us." They were from Holland, and they really had a burden for the Christians in the Communist lands. They said that they named their little girl Emmanuel so that God would always be with them. They had made many trips, and the baby was a great cover for them.

We were told that we were ideal for the work, as we were Americans who travel everywhere for pleasure. We were middle-aged, looking fat, and rich, and it was a perfect cover for the work. We had a third party that was traveling with us, and he was just returning to school. He was a precious black brother from the Ivory Coast of Africa, and he carried no Bibles, as it was his own car and they would have been easily seen. Our Dutch friends were given a white Oldsmobile, and it had secret compartments in the doors and in the wheel wells in the trunk. Both vehicles were loaded with Bibles to the hilt, and no more could be put in any spaces. We also carried suitcases full of clothing of all shapes and sizes for the people that we were being sent to.

We would leave the clothes at the places that could take the Bibles, and they would pass them out.

And so we began our first journey to carry God's word to the suffering people crying and praying for help. We actually went as an answer to many prayers as God later revealed to us, and I am sure that you have felt that way in your life as well. It was such a mixture of feelings that went through us on that first trip: We had excitement, joy, and desire to serve. We were happy that our time had finally come, but truthfully, we also had a great deal of fear of what could happen. We went anyway, and again, it was another course in the college education of God's spiritual school. And remember, *great love gives great courage.*

7e: Culture shock!

The journey was long and exhausting. We traveled down from Vienna, Austria, to Zagreb,

Yugoslavia. My-oh-my, what a tremendous culture shock that was. The road across Yugoslavia was called "Turkey Road." It was a very dangerous stretch of road due to the fact that it was late summer, and all the people were coming home from vacations. I believe that every one of them must have been on that road on the very night that *we* traveled it. It was named Turkey Road due to the Turkish people that swarmed upon it every August.

There were no rest stops as we have here in the United States, and the whole *world* was a rest stop. The people were using the world as a bathroom everywhere we looked. I could not believe it; what a shock to the mind it was. Then, when we had to stop for our *own* needs, every bush already had been used so many times that the whole space was just so polluted. Let me say this, "We watched where we stepped!"

The traffic was bumper-to-bumper, and it was much worse than New York or California freeways. This road was a two-lane road, a killer highway for sure. There were cars along the road on fire from accidents, and cars were coming at us head-on with their lights flashing for us to somehow disappear. There were people out of their cars cursing everyone around for the stalled traffic, and children were crying due to their weariness with the late travel. It was like looking into the bowels of hell, and it took a tremendous toll on Dean to drive so far under such tension. We stopped to eat something, and I fell in the mud, for it had rained. . . . At least, I *think* it was mud, for on that road, it could have been *anything*. Phew! . . . We finally made it.

Our instructions were to go to a crossing point called "Jimbolia" on the Romanian border. Our destination was Timisoara, Romania. We stopped just a few miles from the border to speak with our friends who were traveling with us. We thought that it might be wise to sleep in Yugoslavia that night and cross in the morning, but our African brother said, "We were told we must cross *tonight*." We said, "But we are very tired; it is so late; it would be better to rest and then go on." He insisted, and we did not want to be difficult or argumentative. So we and our Dutch friends agreed: We would cross that night. Dean and I began to praise the Lord, for we knew that there was power in praise, and we needed strength to go on. It was at least 1:00 a.m., and we had traveled many, many tension-filled miles. God came through as always when we praised him, and soon we had a burst of new energy.

We discussed as to who would go first to the border, for we all could not show up at the same time. The border officials would become suspicious with so many crossing at the same time. We agreed that the African brother would go first, and the Dutch couple would go after a short time. Then, Dean and I would go after the Dutch couple had been gone for at least 20 minutes.

Our friend from Africa was being searched so badly when we arrived at the border. They had ripped out the cardboard lining in the trunk, and they had tested all of his tapes and kept the ones that contained any Gospel message. They were looking over all the books that he was taking back to school. It was obvious that his property was being searched thoroughly. He could speak the language, and on the borders, that is not good. In another lane was our dear Dutch friends, and even though they had the baby, it looked like the authorities were still suspicious of them.

We were in the process of being looked over from one end of the camper to the other. We were asked many questions, most in a language that we could not understand, which for a change, was wonderful, for they could not question us as much as they would have liked. We were asked, through motions, if we had any guns, and we replied "No." They saw the many suitcases full of clothes, and they questioned why so many. It came to me to say, "We are Americans; we pack too much." It satisfied their curiosity for the moment. They took lights on poles and looked under the van for secret compartments, and thank God, they could not see the special work that our little Swiss man had done to conceal the word of God. Finally, after much time spent there, they released us.

7f: Behind the Iron Curtain

When we pulled away from the border, the little Dutch couple was being shaken down in a huge way. They were ransacking the car, and the couple and their baby were standing outside the car watching the whole process. We could not linger, or the whole thing would look suspicious. So, we went on, not knowing what we were doing at all. Our African brother was all torn to pieces, and I am sure that they kept him there a very long time. We found out later, when we returned to the mission, that he had been released, and he was back in school minus some tapes, books, and only God knows what else.

I remember very well that on this particular night in August of 1980, it was extremely dark. We drove down a road that was completely lined with flags carrying the hammer and sickle. There were no lights at all along the road to help us see, only our faith and love for God to guide us. We felt the darkness of the country and the feeling of Godlessness in its leaders.

Ceausescu was in authority over the country when we made our journeys into Romania, and he was a very cruel man. He was the General Secretary of the Romanian Communist Party from 1965-1989, and he was the 1st President of Romania from 1974-1989. He created food shortages and tortured many people when he was in office. From 1945 to 1989, more than 2,000,000 people were tortured to death or killed in horrible ways. Ceausescu and his wife were executed in 1989.

It was in Timisoara that the rebellion against the government began, the very city that we had been sent to. What a horrible place it was, and we were very grateful for our country where our faith can be demonstrated on every corner so freely. What a difference in the consciousness of the two countries.

Our instructions were to take the camper to a campground in Timisoara, and from there, the contacts would be made. Our friends would rent a small sleeping place that was available in the campground, and we would go in one vehicle under cover of night to make the deliveries.

Dean and I could not remember the name of the campground where we were to go. We thought that the Dutch couple would lead us, but it didn't happen that way: They could be held at the border all night if the authorities deemed it necessary. We knew that we had to go on alone.

7g: Angels to Guide Us

There were no lights in Timisoara as we approached the city. It was so very dark spiritually and physically. All of a sudden, we saw a taxicab, and we drew up beside it. I rolled the window down and made a tent with my hands, and I said, "Camping, where is camping?" The little driver said, "Hotel, no?" I said again, "No, camping, camping." All the while, I held my hands in the form of a tent. Then, the driver said, "Ah," and he motioned for us to follow him, which we did very willingly. He led us to a campground that was at the outskirts of the city. We thanked him, and he left. We found out later that it was one of many miracles that we would experience, for there were no taxis in Timisoara. We had had an angelic assistance to find our destination.

We registered at the campground, found our spot, and proceeded to go to bed. We arose in the morning, ate a bite of breakfast, washed up a bit, and took a walk around the campground. What a difference from ours here in the United States. We do not know what we have until we make a trip to other lands. There were 2 campgrounds in Timisoara, and we knew that, if we were at the right place, our friends would find us. Otherwise, we would have to move the camper and find the other campground.

Around 10:00 a.m., our Dutch friends found us! They were so thrilled: We had found the right campground, and we had not panicked and left without doing what we had come to do. We said that we would not do that; we had gone through too much to turn back. They, then, told us that they had many Americans who would have done exactly that, and they had seen it happen. We were feeling ashamed for the others that could have done that, but we all must answer to God in the end, so we cannot judge them. We knew that we must accomplish what we were sent to do. It seemed that our friends had run out of gas in the middle of the night, and so they had lost touch with us.

We proceeded to make our plans for that night. We would have to pull the camper into the woods where we would not be seen, open the floor, and take out the Bibles. We would, then, place them in suitcases, and when the contact would be made where the Bibles could be accepted, we would deliver the camperful of light and life to many. The Dutch couple would have to do the same with their car. It was tricky business, and it had to be done secretly, quietly, and quickly. We went back into the woods with our camper and proceeded to do the procedure that opened the floor so that we could gain access to the Bibles. I remember how tense we were as we worked quickly, and I held watch for Dean, as he had to get on his knees and reach from one side to the other to make sure that he got them all. We finally finished that step of the job, closed the floor up, and breathed a big sigh of relief. Now, it was time to make the contact.

7h: Our First Visit to the Suffering Church

Dean and I were chosen to make the first contact, and it had to be done under the cover of darkness in Romania. There were no streetlights, and it was unbelievable how very dark it was in a city where no light was available. Our Dutch friends dropped us off about 2 blocks from the address, and they waited in the car until we could be sure that it was safe. I remember my heart, and I am sure my husband's heart as well, beating very fast, for we were breaking a law in a foreign country for the first time in our lives; and it could have meant *prison* if we had been caught. We were both raised in very law-abiding homes, and this was a completely new experience. God's laws always supersede man's laws, and we knew that we were operating in *God's* laws: He had called us, and there was no doubt that we would do his will.

We had no light of any kind to help us see the house numbers, so we had to get right up to the house and strain to see the number. We didn't want to draw attention to ourselves in such a place, for we were operating illegally and could have brought trouble to the people that we were seeking. We came to a house that we felt might be it, but it wasn't. We knew that we were close, and so we walked a bit further and checked again, and this time it was the right house. All the windows were very dark, and it looked as though no one was home. Dean said, "There is no one here," and I said, "We will knock anyway." I remember well reaching up and tapping lightly on the door. All of a sudden, the door opened, and a hand reached out. Then we heard, "Hallelujah, hallelujah." They knew immediately that we were God's people from the West, and we must have something great for them. We were hugged warmly and greeted in Romanian, which we felt was full of love, but we could not understand them. They went to their phone and called their son, who could speak perfect English. He bicycled across town to come and speak to us.

7i: We Give Spiritual Food; They Give Us Their Best

The Dutch couple was waiting for us, so after the son arrived and everyone understood our visit better, Dean and I returned to the car and said, "They can still receive the Bibles." The couple helped us to deliver the suitcases full of Bibles, and then they went back to the car to wait. We would never leave the believers without eating with them. They got out their best cloth and best dishes, which were chipped, but they were the best they had. They all went in and changed their clothes for us. They put on their best clothes, for the American pastors had come. I don't remember what we ate. I had never eaten it before or since. It was not bad tasting, just different. We had a wonderful talk with these very precious people that night. One of the men could not speak our language, and he wanted to convey to us his heartfelt thoughts. He brought his Bible to us and opened it up to a place in 1 Thess. 3:7-9, "Therefore, brethren, we were comforted over you in all our affliction and distress by your faith: For now we live, if ye stand fast in the Lord. For what thanks can we render to God again for you, for all the joy wherewith we joy for your sakes before our God; . . ." We were deeply moved by this man's love and his word to us.

We ate their food and listened (through the son) to what they were facing there. The son said he was amazed that:

1. We were American.
2. We were pastors.
3. We knew about their suffering.

We said, "We know, Bother, we know." Our response changed his attitude about us here in the United States.

When we poured out the 250 Bibles, they ran their hands over them so lovingly, and they said, "This is good. . . . "Is this all you brought?" We said, "Yes, it was all that would fit in our camper." They were disappointed, for they knew so many who needed a Bible. When I heard that, I remembered how readily we could go to a store (in the U.S) and buy a Bible with ease. Over there, it was a different story: It was so very *precious* there, for it was so very scarce.

And so we ate, cried, laughed, shared our faith, hugged them all again, and blessed them. Then we said a few more hallelujahs to each other and departed for the West. We left with a heart full and running over of love for them and for all those who were like them. What a tremendous chance they took in handing out the Bibles. Their lives were in jeopardy every time they shared one of them, but they continued to do it anyway. Oh, what great courage they demonstrated to us that night.

It is so hard to explain fully just what we felt in our obedience to the Lord to do this kind of work. What a fulfillment in our lives in such a way we had never experienced before. We saw a *beauty* in these people that we never had seen before, for suffering brings out the beauty. What a joy, and I do mean joy, to bring them such a gift they had prayed so much for. How great is our God! In the Communist lands, it took every cent to feed them, and so clothes were nearly impossible to purchase. We were told that the women would own one winter coat in a lifetime, and that is a long time to wear one coat. We left them money, hopefully to purchase some clothing for themselves.

Many times, in years before, Dean and I had always been drawn to the suffering Church. We had read many books that had been published on the subject like *"God's smuggler,"* *"Brother Andrew,"* and books by Wurmbrand from Romania, like *"Tortured for Christ,"* etc. We always had a burden and an interest in the people of God who have no freedom in their worship of the Lord. Now, here we were, taking Bibles to these precious folks. It was a fulfillment that eased the burden that we had carried so long.

We returned to the car, joined our friends, and returned to the campground for the night. After a good night's rest, we began to make plans for Jaap, Jeanette, and little Emmanuel to make *their* contact in the afternoon. We rode passed the house whose residents were to receive the Bibles. Later on, we drove the white Oldsmobile, which by now had all the Bibles from the secret compartments transferred into suitcases. Our friends had us park about 2 blocks from the home where the Bibles would be taken. It would be *our* turn to wait while *they* made the delivery.

7j: Danger Lurks Near

We found a place to park and waited for them while they went to see if the Bibles could be delivered to the address they had. They went by foot to speak to the people about receiving the material, and we began our wait for them to let us know the next step in the plan.

All of a sudden, I felt that something was very wrong. I started to look around as I said to Dean, "Something is wrong. I don't know what, but I feel very upset in my spirit." I have always been very intuitive, and I could feel or see things in the Spirit for a lot of my life. It was in full-speed that day, and I was looking everywhere, for I felt that we were in danger. All of a sudden, I looked up, and there, on a guard tower that we had chosen to park beside, was a guard looking down with a gun in his hands. I saw him coming down the ladder, and I said to Dean, "Oh-oh, he is coming to the car." He came to Dean's window and looked in. Now remember, we had suitcases full of Bibles in the trunk, and they could have been discovered very easily if he had decided to look around. He spoke to us, in Romanian, a message that we could not understand. We said, "We are American, we speak English." Then, in perfect English, he said, "Go from this place, great danger here, great danger here." Needless to say, he did not have to tell us twice. Dean had a terrible time starting the car, for we were more than a little tense at that moment. Finally, the car kicked in, and we drove away as quickly as we could.

Then, we had a problem, for our friends had left us in *one* place, and now we had to move the car. It occurred to me to drive the car on a street that we knew they would have to pass to find us again, and when we would see them, I would get out of the car and very quietly tell them that we had to move the car. Everything would have to be done as carefully and as casually as possible.

Later, when I saw them coming, I left the car and walked up to them. I whispered the message, and they followed me back to the car. We all agreed that it was another miracle from God to keep us safe from harm, for if the authorities had opened the trunk and opened the suitcases, we could have been in big trouble.

When our friends had the chance to talk, they told us that their contacts could not receive the Bibles. More than likely, they were being watched from past activities, etc.; we did not know why. They just told our friends that they were not free to receive them, so we decided to take them to the people who had received the Bibles from Dean and me the previous night.

Later that night, the suitcases full of Bibles were delivered, and the precious people fed our brother and sister with their very best. They were rejoicing that the whole load of God's word was left with them, for they had many places to give them. Now, we were free to leave this very heavy, dark place. We might have been just a small part of planting the word of God that gave the people of Timisoara, Romania the courage to rebel against their leadership. I believe we were.

7k: We Leave Romania . . . Gladly!

By next morning, we were ready to leave Romania, and we were all more than ready to do so, for the darkness was heavy on all of us, and it made even our *body* weary to stay in those places very long. It was an energy-drainer, not a life-giver.

On our way out of the country, we were heading for the border when our friends were pulled over by the Romanian police. By this time, we had rid ourselves of any evidence that would tell why we were in the country. The police told our friend that

201

he needed to go to the police station, but he couldn't understand them very well, for he did not speak their language. He became very angry, and in his own language, he told them that he had broken no laws and he would not go anywhere with them. He, then, got into his car and started for the border. We were parked by the road and waiting for them, for we were not leaving without them. The police in those Communist countries would often stop Westerners and *fine* them so they could get more of their money before they left for the West.

We proceeded to leave again, and on the way out, we passed a bakeshop, and we were hungry. I said, "Stop, I will buy us some goodies to eat." Dean pulled in, and I went in and purchased a few very brown sweet-looking rolls. I had my mouth all set, for they looked very good, but what a shock! They were *horrible* to say the least! There was not enough shortening, so they were very *tough*, not *flaky* like ours here. In addition, there was not enough *sugar*, so they tasted like flour and water. What a disappointment they were to us, and so we chewed for a while and threw the rest away.

When we got through Yugoslavia again and entered Austria, we were driving along, and we could smell food cooking. It was chicken, cooking on the spit in a restaurant by the road. I will never forget how wonderful it smelled and tasted. After 3 days of eating in the Eastern Bloc countries, we were ready for some good food from the West, and it was a meal that we will never forget. Chicken never tasted so good before or since. It was heavenly!

71: Back to the Mission

We returned to the mission and had couple days of rest. Then, we were asked to make another journey, this time to *Hungary*. Our Dutch friends were returning to their home in Holland, for they had finished their time with the mission for that year. There was another couple in the mission at the time named Ben and Marian. They were from Belgium. We were asked to travel with them, and we agreed. We began to prepare for the trip: We laid out maps, received money for the trip, and purchased the food for the journey.

I remember that one of the things we purchased was a burpless cucumber. Why I bought it, I don't know, but it would be our entire dinner-for-four on the night that we would make our contact. We were given one contact only for that trip. The contact was a pastor who walked with the Bibles to the Russian soldiers under cover of night. He would pass out the Bibles and share his faith. There was a revival that was going on amongst the Russian soldiers.

7m: Russian Tanks Pass Us

Before we went to the pastor's home, we were going to pray first. We were all in the camper, as I recall, and we women were in the back. We had pulled off the road (a short distance from the pastor's home) to have our prayer time. We had our eyes closed during the prayer, yet we were aware of a lot of noise. None of us looked up during the entire prayer. Then, after the prayer, the men said, "Now, *that* was really *something*." They asked us women, "Do you know what the noise was?" We said "No." They said, "20 Russian tanks just passed us with their guns up." We said, "Now, *that* was a very good place to pray." There was a base nearby, and we had chosen to pray right next to it. It just so happened that the base was the same one that the little pastor visited with the Bibles.

It is strange, but I do not recall many details of that trip. I do remember that we all went together to make the contact. We approached the pastor's house very carefully, and the other couple knocked on his door. The pastor took one look and said, "Pull your auto very quickly behind my home." He had a setup where we backed right into the garage and unloaded the Bibles under cover of the garage so that his neighbors would not be suspicious. We had such a sweet visit with him, and he was so glad to get the Bibles. He asked us, "Where have you been?" He then explained that it had been 10 months since he had received any shipment, and he needed them badly. We told him that we knew nothing about all that, as we had just gotten there.

He made us some coffee that kept me awake all night: It was so strong that I believe the spoon almost stood alone in it. He also served us some very stale pretzels and some very small stale bits of chocolate. He wanted to do something special, and in that country, it was very special. We found out later that, every time a trip was planned to go to him, either the people backed out or something else would come up, and he would be left to wait again. So much love and appreciation was felt from these very wonderful people. We came away, again, fulfilled in a very deep way in our souls.

7n: A Prayer Is Answered

Again, we returned to the mission; and again, there was a delay for the next trip. It was about this time that Martin-and-Bella and Dean-and-I were having a time of fellowship after supper one night. Martin began to unload his heart to us about a lot of inner conflicts that he had over many things. He got very honest about some very personal things, and through the Spirit of God and the gifts of the Spirit,

207

we were able to help this brother with some very deep inner healing. He was so relieved and so thankful for our coming. He said, "God sent you all this way just for me." Praise the Lord. He loves us all so very much. He does those kind of things. Martin was seeking answers, and God had given those answers to us to help him come into peace in his life.

7o: One More Trip

It was about this time that Bella herself wanted to make a trip with Dean and me. So the three of us were assigned a trip into Yugoslavia together. Again, we were given maps, money, and contacts to deliver the Bibles. We were given only one contact for this trip, for all the Bibles would go to that one place. The woman that would receive them had the ability to get them to where they needed to go.

Again, we were traveling, and this time to Yugoslavia. The borders there were not as difficult as some of the others, and we crossed them easily. We traveled quite a ways on the first day, and it began to be later in the day. We decided to stop at what they call a "motel" of sorts. Dean and I were in one room, and Bella was in another room a little ways down the hall. We carried bread and cheese most of the time: It didn't spoil; it filled us up; it took no preparation time; and it was readily available to purchase in Austria. We ate it everywhere we went.

7p: The Archangel Michael

After eating a small lunch, we settled on the sides of the twin beds. I always was uneasy in my spirit in those Communist lands. We were reading our Bibles when, all of a sudden, I felt a *presence* in the room, and it was not *God*. I looked up toward

209

the little hallway through which we had entered the room, and there stood one of the largest dark figures that I have ever seen. God told me not to fear, for everything was under control. I, then, noticed *another* figure in the room: It was a huge angel. I believe that it was the Archangel Michael. He walked toward the dark figure and raised a flaming sword, and the darkness departed. It was God's awesome protection in those places. God told us, that night, that he had sent the angel whenever we had done that kind of work to keep us safe. Now, if we had seen the angel on *that* night, how many times had our loving heavenly Father sent it at *other* times without our awareness? How great is his love.

The next morning, we left for the contact's house. We still had a long way to go, and on the way, it became lunchtime. There was some kind of eating-place along the road, and it had *hamburgers* on the menu. We believed that we perfectly understood what was on the menu, and we remarked, "What wrong can anyone possibly do to a *burger*?" Well, we were soon to see. . . . All of a sudden (after only a few minutes), out came the largest, greasiest-looking piece of hamburger that I had ever seen. The wrapping was soaked with grease; it was *everywhere*. It turned me off so badly that I could not eat it. I tasted a small bite, and I don't think that it was beef at all; it had to be more like *horsemeat*, etc. Anyway, I couldn't eat it. On the other hand, Dean and Bella did quite well with theirs.

We left there and continued on our mission.

7q: Where He Leads Me, I Will Follow; What He Feeds Me, I Will Swallow!

We made the contact that night. Bella was skilled in many languages, so she could speak to the lovely lady where we left the Bibles. Their conversation was very animated and enjoyable for them, but it was very *limited* for Dean and me, for Bella had to interpret for us. The lady was wonderful, and again, out came the best cloth, the best dishes, etc. The woman opened up a canned meat-product of some kind, and I took one look and could tell that it was full of *gristle*. I have never been able to *handle* that sort of food: Here in the United States, such food would be considered as a *waste product*, not food.

I said to Bella, "Do I have to eat that?" She said, "You must." I said, "But what if I can't hold it down?" She replied, "You will eat it, and you will hold it down. If you don't, you will offend these people very deeply." I gulped and said, "Okay, I will try my best." I remember eating small bites and not chewing very much. I bolted it pretty much like a dog would. She was giving us her very best, and to deny it, would have been *hurtful* to her. We delivered the Bibles and enjoyed the fellowship with her; and again, we hugged her and said our goodbyes. Every delivery was a unique experience; no two were alike.

Let me say here that every song we have ever sung, whether in Church or at meetings where the Holy Spirit was present and dealing with our heart, became a promise or vow to God. He reminded us of all the times that we stood and sang, "Where he leads me I will follow, I'll go with him, with him, all the way." God told us that he was holding us to that promise. The song should really go, "Where he leads me I will follow, what he feeds me I will swallow." Those were the real testing times as well, just as we had faced here in Yugoslavia.

We spent another night in Yugoslavia, and the next day, we headed for Vienna, Austria, the mission headquarters where we were staying. With every trip we made, we were filled with joy. We knew that we were fulfilling the call that we had heard, and we were deeply contented with our lives. We were many miles from home, being challenged on every side and filled with fear many times as we crossed borders, but we were also very fulfilled with each trip and with each contact that we made. What an awesome God that we serve. He surely knows what brings joy to us if we will only listen.

7r: We Become Tourists for a Day

By this time, our stay was coming to a close in Europe. In a few days, we would have to pack up and get on a train that would carry us back to Berlin, Germany, where we would fly back to the States. During these few days, Martin decided to take a car and ask us to go with him to Vienna. He wanted to show us a few of the wonderful sights there. We agreed, and one morning, we drove into the real tourist areas in Vienna.

We were taken to a huge Church, completely built of stone. It seemed that it must have been as large as half-a-city-block. It had a huge steeple, lovely stained glass windows, and a huge pipe organ that filled the front. We could tell, by its appearance, that many, many feet had walked over those stones for many years. As they say, "If walls could talk, what a tale could be told." There were many pews in the building, very well worn, but truly lovely. The place was very large, very old, and very beautiful, but the presence of God was more powerful in the believer's homes where we had delivered the Bibles than in this Church. It was a huge tourist attraction. We enjoyed the opportunity to view it, and we were grateful to our Brother Martin for taking us there.

Then, Martin wanted us to see another place that was very famous and unusual in Vienna. It happened to be where many planes were built during the Second World War, and it was all underground. It was *huge*! I don't remember the statistics, but there were some of the old planes still in this underground garage when we toured it. It was hard to believe that all the dirt had to be carried out, and it had to be braced up so it wouldn't cave in. To us, it was an engineering miracle. It was so large that planes could pass each other inside. Many were built there, and no one saw what was going on.

We were very impressed with our day in Vienna. We ate out, bought a few small souvenirs to bring back, and returned to the mission tired, happy, and blessed.

7s: We Meet the Head of the Mission

The day before we had to leave for Berlin, the head of the entire mission asked Martin to bring us to meet him. We were told that this was very unusual, for he was an extremely busy man, and he didn't usually communicate with those that came to do the journeys. He had heard about us: He knew our age; we were Americans; and we didn't panic. He was *impressed*, I think. We went to meet him, and when we arrived, he shook our hands and asked us to sit down. He, then, began to question us about where we lived in the States, our family, and how we had heard of the mission. He was very interested in just how we had come. I said, "Do you have some time?" He said, "Yes, I do." I shortened the story as much as I could, and basically I told him that *God* had spoken to us, and we obeyed. He was very touched by our story, and he said, "I can see God in

217

your lives." He thanked us for coming and invited us back, letting us know that they would always be glad to see us again.

While we were with him, he gave us some interesting statistics about the mission: In June and July of that year, 45,000 and 40,000 pieces of Christian literature crossed over Communist borders from that mission alone. That was just from one mission alone. He said that, in all the trips that were made in 10 years, only *two* were stopped due to the people panicking, and they were Americans. I felt embarrassed for all of us Americans. Nevertheless, with these facts, we can see just how much work was being done to help the suffering Church. All we can say is, "Praise our great God for his high and wondrous ways."

In our great God's plan and wisdom, there are no borders or divisions that can keep his Spirit out of any land. The only borders or separations that can keep God's Spirit out is in our minds. Man's thinking is what creates the walls of misunderstanding that keep us apart. It is never *God* that does these things.

After meeting the director of the mission, it was soon time to leave all of our newfound friends: They were friends we had made in the mission, friends who had traveled with us, and friends we had left behind the Iron Curtain. It was a happy and sad day for us. We were very happy and fulfilled in all we had been able to accomplish while on this mission, but we were also sad to be leaving so many who needed so much. For this time in our lives, this chapter was over.

We did not feel that this call for Communist lands had been fulfilled completely. So, with a mixture of feelings, we climbed on the train that would take us back to Berlin, and from there, we would board a plane that would take us back home to the United States.

Chapter 8: Ministries Closer to Home

8a: We Return Home to Another Challenge

Our flight seemed long, tiring, and always seemed to put us into jetlag. I will never forget how I felt when we arrived at home: When we got off the plane, I wanted to kiss the ground of this great country. How I love my homeland, even though it is not perfect. When Dean and I travel, we easily notice that our country is far better than anything we ever had seen. We did enjoy Austria and the other free areas that we had visited, but our hearts were full of *gratefulness* as we arrived in the United States. I felt very emotional upon standing on American soil again.

When we finally arrived at our little home, it seemed so strange to us: Our children who had been living with us had moved out. Many of the rooms were empty, and we had to move our bedroom furniture down stairs again and re-arrange a number of things. We did not know, then, just where they had moved, but we found out later. In our hearts, we wished them well, and we moved on into the next phase of our lives.

We began to receive calls for us to come and speak about our journey overseas, and we began to be very busy. We began to be away a lot of the time, and so our home would sit empty for long periods of time. Once, we arrived home after being gone for a short time, and our neighbors told us that they saw someone trying to break into our home, and they stopped them. When we heard this, we realized that we could not be everywhere. We could not be on the road doing God's work and be concerned over our home's safety. God began to challenge us again about lessening the burden of possessions. He spoke loud and clear to Dean and me, and he told us to sell it all and get on the road for him.

At that time, we had been married over 25 years and had accumulated a lot of things. We had gotten rid of a lot of things in the move from Wadhams Road to 13th Street, but we still had a lot of just plain *stuff*. We began to call people we knew and tell our close friends and family about the next move in our lives. We listed the house with the same realtor we had used to find the home in the beginning and placed it in the hands of God. In just a few short weeks, it sold. We had been out ministering the word in Canada, and when we came home, the phone rang. I picked it up, and it was the realtor that had been trying to get ahold of us about an offer he had for our home. We accepted the offer and emptied our home as God had ordered; and in just a month or so, it all was over for us and our ownership of a home.

The last week in our home, Dean and I slept in sleeping bags on the floor of our bedroom. It was a very strange feeling to watch everything that we had ever gained in this life materially walk out the door. It was also very freeing as well. Stuff is bondage as well as a blessing, and we knew that we were in the perfect will of God, and that is what brought us great comfort.

When we closed the deal on our home, we went and bought a van and a small house trailer to travel with and live in when we would be in town. When it was cold, we stayed in my parents' house in their extra bedroom. My mother at that time served as our secretary, and we used her phone and her address as the ministries' place of contact. It all fell into place as God said it would, and there was very little money left after making those two purchases, but we were peaceful and content in his will.

By this time, the Christmas Season had come, and we were in my parents' home for that. We had one call for ministry to Sidney, Ohio in January, and we were waiting for the timing to leave for that meeting. In the meantime, my parents had some very close friends in Fort Worth, Texas, and Dean and I bought them some airline tickets so they could enjoy the warmer weather for at least a couple of weeks. The day we left for Sidney, Ohio, we took them to the airport in Detroit to catch their flight to Texas. It happened to be a day when God decided to dump a lot of snow in a short time. I remember very well sitting in the Metropolitan Airport, watching it snow and snow. We couldn't leave, as we had carried my parents to the airport and knew that we had to wait to see them leave so they wouldn't be left in the airport with no one to take them home if the flight was cancelled.

8b: The Days of Traveling Begin

The day drew on; the snow kept falling; and we kept praying for God to release the plane for my parents' flight. We watched the large snowplows all day, plowing the runways over and over. Finally, late in the day, they called my parents' flight number, and we said our goodbyes. They were off to warmth, and we were off to find a motel so we could start out in the morning when the roads would be clearer.

We located one nearby. We paid way too much for it, but we went to bed anticipating the next stage in our journey for the Lord here at home. We left the next morning, which was a typical January day: It was bright, beautiful, and very, very cold with lots of snow. We had a good trip to Sidney, Ohio. When we arrived at our destination, we thought that it would be just for a few meetings, but God had another idea.

We stayed with a very sweet lady, and she did her best to make us comfortable. We slept on a fold-out couch in her living room. Her home was very cold, and I remember needing more blankets in the night. She was quite poor, and some of the other people helped her to supply us with food while we were there. She was very hospitable to us, and we labored in that area for over a week. We held home meetings, and we had a very good response spiritually, but we were being challenged by the Lord there, for we did not receive any offerings. Everyone seemed to be on welfare or in need themselves, and so we blessed them with the word, our love, and our prayers.

While we were in Sidney, Ohio, we heard about a convention that was being held. We felt to attend, and so we went to these special meetings. They went on for close to a week. We did not preach or teach there; we only attended the meetings. At the last meeting, which was at the end of the week, the lady minister that we had met there wanted to speak to us: From the front of the Church, she said that she wanted to see us before we left the Church that night. We went to her after the meeting and asked her what she might be wanting us for. She handed us an envelope with $800.00 in it, and she said that it was a love offering for us. Isn't God so awesome to us? The other place where we worked so hard could not give, so God made up for it in *this* place. We felt that it was the offering from the *first* week's work. We said so many thank-you and hallelujahs to her and God. How great are his ways, so very high.

We moved along again. In those meetings that we had just come from, we met another pastor who invited us to come and speak. This happened to us so many times that it is impossible to remember them all and where they all were. God planned our itinerary for sure. We left in January for one meeting, and it was almost 6 months later before we got back home. That is how our entire road ministry went. We truly went by faith, for one door would open and another would open from that, etc. What a wonderful time of trust and dependence on God we had, and it really has not changed much.

Of course, I remember some Churches in particular, for they stand out in our minds for many reasons. I spoke in many women's groups and retreats. We always knew who was supposed to speak when we arrived in a place. God would speak to us and say, "*Dean* should speak, for this is a place where women would not be accepted." Then, there were places where *I* would be the speaker. We always just waited on God, and he would let us know just who would be more readily accepted.

I remember going to a women's morning meeting. It was either a Church of God or Assembly of God; I do not remember exactly which organization it was. It was a group that knew about the *baptism* of the Spirit and the *gifts* of the Spirit, but they were not aware of the *power* of those gifts. I remember that very well. I was in front of the Church preaching, and all of a sudden, the Spirit of God came upon me, and the word of knowledge and word of wisdom began to operate through me.

I began to point to certain women and bring a word of encouragement to them. It was a word of knowledge that I personally would not have known, but God knew them, and he told me what to say. Nothing I said was anything that should have embarrassed them or made them feel guilty. It was a tremendous time of God's Spirit, and I was as surprised as they were. Some came forward and asked me different questions, and the Spirit gave me answers for them.

At the end of the meeting, we were on our way out, and the pastor's wife said on the steps of the Church, "I sure am glad you did not see anything for me." Then, the Lord spoke to me and told me that she was very frightened of what I was seeing and that she *did* have some things she was hiding. I never would have brought out what I saw about her in a public meeting, for God is a gentleman. We were never invited back there, which did not surprise us.

In our travels and in our entire ministry, we have seen a paradox with people: They want God's presence in the meetings; they pray that he will speak to the people; they ask for all sorts of things. Then, when it begins to happen, they begin to run and hide from his presence. God is a God of love, and he loves us all so very much and wants only the best for us. His presence makes demands on our lives though, and he comes to us for many reasons. We are allowed to experience his presence so that we might know he is very real. He has a plan for every life, and our flesh wants to run from his will, for it is hard on the flesh many times. It makes us uncomfortable to experience the tremendous power of his presence; and how sad that is for us. We should be rejoicing that he would grace us with his presence.

I remember another lady minister that we worked with. She asked us to minister in her Church, and upon our arrival, God told me that I had the message. We arrived as we usually do, well in advance of the meeting time. The people began to gather, and we all sat and waited and waited and waited. I asked a couple of times where the minister was, and they said, "Oh, she is *always* late." I asked, "*How* late?" They said they never knew. She was just upstairs in her office, and I could not understand how, as a leader, she could put her people out by being so late to her own meeting.

She finally arrived at least one hour late, and we held the meeting. The people were very special and extremely open and desirous of the word. This person had a number of Churches that she was head of. She asked us back for a women's retreat, and we came. I went with the women, and Dean stayed with a lady's husband from the Church. The minister, who was always late, had planned way too much for the day at the retreat, and she insisted that she would have it all happen anyway. Just let me say this: It did not happen. We were running from one thing to another all day, and because she was so late to start, we never got it all in. I knew that I would never go back to anything like that again. Before we left, she asked me if I would go to one of her Churches to stand up and prophesy what she would give me to say to set those people straight. I refused immediately and completely, and I told her that *God* tells Dean and me what to say, no one else. I *could* not and *would* not ever do what she was asking. She, then, told us that, if we would do what she said, she would keep us busy forever; and we would be well taken care of with finance. That was our last time to be with this person. We moved on.

We had a wonderful woman in Jasper, Arkansas; we stayed with her a lot. She was very hungry for God; she had no husband; and her door was always open to us. Many times, we would take our trailer and set it up in her yard, and we would stay and preach in her home. We went on a 21-day fast with her at one time. It was a very challenging time for all of us, but God blessed us mightily for it. This dear sister has since passed over. While we were in her life, she met a wonderful man, for God gave her a soul mate, and she lived the last years of her life with a lot of love. Dean and I were privileged to do the wedding for her. She was a very special person that God used while we were on the road. We travel north, south, east, and west.

We did a lot of work in Missouri, Texas, Oklahoma, Ohio, Indiana, New York, Pennsylvania, etc. We traveled into Canada as well: Saskatchewan, Manitoba, and Ontario.

We had many journeys into the Philippines, Haiti, and of course, all over Europe. Little did we know that, when we were being raised so humbly on our small farms, we would someday put all these miles on our lives. God had a plan, and we said "Yes."

On one of our trips, we were invited to do a number of speaking engagements in Saskatchewan, Canada. It was late March when we were there, and there was snow piled over the fence posts yet in that area, as spring takes longer to arrive that far north. We went to many Churches in that province and had a week-long invitation to a Spirit-filled Church there. We arrived on a Saturday and went to the Church that we had been invited to. When we arrived, we were met by some ladies, and we were shown to a room in the basement of the Church where we would be staying while we were with them. They also showed us the kitchen in the basement where we could prepare our own meals.

We were genuinely *shocked* at this, as most of the time, someone would open their homes and feed us; so this was a real departure from the normal. We thanked them and then asked where the nearest laundromat was. They gave us directions, and we said our goodbyes for that day.

We proceeded to find the laundromat and wash the clothes before returning to the Church where we were staying. We settled in and prepared to minister the next morning, which was Sunday. Dean would speak in the morning service, and I would minister in the evening service. This Church believed that women should not minister without wearing a hat, so I had gone to one of our second-hand stores and purchased one just for this occasion. I knew that I would never wear it again, so I did not want to pay a lot of money for it. It was a neutral-color hat, black. It could be worn with *anything,* so I felt that I was ready for this challenge. Neither Dean nor I was feeling very well that evening, but we went ahead with the preparation for the services anyway.

The next morning, we showered, ate breakfast, and went upstairs to the service. We were really beginning to feel much sicker by this point, but others were depending on us. So we did a lot of praying and went ahead anyway.

The service began with Sunday school, which was taught by the pastor of the Church -- oh, how *dead* it was; there was nothing more dead! Then, the Spirit filled those who had lost their first love for

God. It was just *dreadful* to say the least. We endured it all, and then *Dean* got up to preach. He was beginning to run a fever by now; and he asked, from the pulpit, for the people to pray for him. This was a Church that believed in "laying on of hands" for healing, but no one responded to Dean's request. We felt no love there at all during the whole time that we were there. It was a very hard time for us. The basement was cold, and so were the people. We had no control of the heat, so we could not turn it up. We were ill, and that made us feel colder anyway.

The plan for our time of ministry was that, every night of the week, we were to be taken by van to different locations around the area to minister. Some of the areas were on reservations, although we were in Church buildings where we went. Monday night came, and we were really feeling pretty awful by then. We both had been vomiting, and our fevers were higher for certain. We stayed in bed all day, and when someone came in to do something in the building, we asked him to contact a doctor for us. He told us that no one would take us, for we were out-of-town people. We thanked him and went back to bed.

We got up in time to dress and get ready for the trip to the location for us to minister. We would be traveling into Manitoba that evening for the meeting. The people, that came to pick us up, took one look at us and said that we didn't look too good. We told them that we sure didn't *feel* very good either. We got in the van, and along the way, I shouted, "Stop the van, I am going to be sick!" They pulled over, and I had told the truth. We had not eaten anything, so thank God for *that*. I was supposed to preach that night, and I did. I was never so glad to finish in my whole life. We were taken back to the cold basement, where Dean and I prepared for bed. The next night, we went through the whole ordeal again. We were to do one more night of this, and I told Dean that I couldn't take any more: We went to the emergency room of the hospital nearby.

We gave our names and explained that we had no insurance. We also explained that we were in ministry, and we were responsible for a week's meetings in a near-by Church. The reception nurse told us to sign our names, and she would see if one of the doctors could look at us. I could see, by the many people in the waiting room, that it would be a long wait. Fortunately, however, we did not wait long. When our names were called, we explained our symptoms, and the doctor took our temperature and listened to our heart and lungs. He, then, told us that there was a *virus* going around. I told him that we were in ministry; we had no insurance; and we had been on the road for many months preaching and teaching. He gave us a prescription to have filled, and he told us that he was not charging us anything for *his* part, but he was not sure of what the *hospital* would charge us. He also told us that we would not get well without rest, and he advised us to cancel the rest of the meetings and go somewhere to rest until we were well.

We were greatly relieved to hear this news, as we were very sick. We were very weak, feverish, vomiting, aching, and all the other nasty symptoms one could have at one time. I believe that we were run down from the many beds and many miles that we had traveled. It was a great prescription for us, as we felt very much like our time there had not accomplished much. We were ready to head back to the States again.

We returned to the Church, and some people were there. So we told them what had happened and what the doctor had said. They seemed relieved that we were leaving and we would not be in their Church basement anymore. They also seemed glad that they would not need to take us out at night anywhere, and they agreed readily with the doctor's instructions.

During our stay there, no one brought us anything to eat, not even a can of soup. They did not stop by when they knew that we were ill. One day, we got up so sick that it was a *struggle* to go out and buy some chicken soup to make us feel a bit better. In all our times of ministry, we had *never* been so neglected or ignored as we were in that Church. There was no testimony there as to the love of God or his care through his people.

We packed up very quickly and proceeded to head for the United States border. We immediately, began to feel better, just knowing that we would be out of that cold basement and out of that cold-hearted Church. We went as far as we could that same day, and that was a long way for us in our condition. We wanted to sleep in the United States that night, and so we really had to push it physically to do that.

We stayed in Montana that night and for another day and night after that. It was amazing to us that we felt so much better as we entered our own country again. Now, you must understand: We do not have anything against Canadians, as some of our most blessed times have been with the Canadian people. They had always been warm, receptive, encouraging, willing to feed us and provide lodging for us. So this experience was such a disappointment to us, and it was a very rare moment in all of our years of road ministry.

We often went to a wonderful lady in Oklahoma. She was always willing to open her home to us. She was all alone in a large home, and she worked out every day. Yet, nothing was too much for her.

Whenever we stayed at someone's home, we always did what we could to help out: We washed clothes, washed dishes, helped prepare meals, etc. Whatever we saw to do, we did.

During this period, we always had different people traveling with us to train in ministry. God would bring them across our path, and we would feel that we were to take them with us. When we did, we always paid for their expenses. Most of them were very needy, but they felt a call to go out and be of some help to others. We took many to the

Philippines and Haiti, and we paid their full expenses. We don't regret anything that we ever did. We had a vision, and we wanted to share it with others.

8c: Too Much Pressure

When we would be in Port Huron, we had to stay at my parents' home, even with these others. It was a small home, and it was very crowded. It put a lot of pressure on my folks. Although my mom handled it beautifully, my father was beginning to go into the first stages of Alzheimer's disease, and he could not take it anymore.

One Sunday, we were at the table eating, and he blew up and told us that we had to get out, as he could not stand it. So, the meal being ruined, we began to pack. We had nowhere to go, and we had another lady living with us at that time. Then, we remembered a young woman that we had ministered to. She had been sharing an apartment with another person who had recently moved out. It was a 3-bedroom apartment, just a short ways from my parents' home. We called her and said that we had to move on that same day, and she told us to come ahead. We would be helping her with the rent, etc., and she needed the help. She worked afternoons at a nursing home, and she would be gone until after 11:00 p.m. every day. We moved in that day.

The next day, we called the landlord and told him that we needed a home. We explained that the other girl had agreed to our sharing the expenses with her if it was okay with him. He was wonderful. He said, "I don't care how many live there as long as you maintain it." So again, our God took care of our needs in a wonderful way. Our share of the expenses was $125.00, and that included everything but the phone bill. We had a new address, and my parents had some freedom and their space back.

Chapter 9: Back to Europe

9a: God Calls Again

About this time, we had left to go back out on the road again to hold a group of meetings in many places. We were driving along, and I had a vision: I saw us in a small car driving through mountains, and I knew that God was saying that we were going back to Europe. I felt that it was our next trip to Communist lands, as we had both been picking up a burden for the Polish people, and we wondered how it would all happen.

I spoke out what I saw to Dean, and he witnessed to it. We knew that if God had spoken, it would come to pass, and it did. It wasn't long before we began to share the burden as we traveled, and we began to gather the offerings toward it. The couple that had been our hosts in the mission house in Austria had moved to Switzerland, and we had been corresponding regularly with them. I wrote to them to share our vision and our burden for the Polish people, and they were very positive about our coming and staying with them in Winterthur, Switzerland. They knew of a Church that would not only give us a Toyota van to drive, but they would also fill it with things for the people if we would take it in. So, once more, little by little, the arrangements were made for our trip behind the Iron Curtain.

At the time that we were being led to go, the Polish people were suffering so much from lack of food as well as other needs. Our friends, Martin and Bella, told us that many were getting across the borders without searches at that time, and so they encouraged us to come, and they would arrange things for us. We had a woman whom we had met in our journeys, and she expressed a desire to accompany us on the trip. She said that she felt the Spirit of God calling her to go, and so we agreed. We asked Bella if she could put up one more guest, and she said that it would be all right, and she would make room for the extra guest.

This was in 1982, just 2 years after the other trip. We left on September 8, and we flew out of Toronto, Canada. We arrived on Sept 9, and our friends were there to meet us in Zurich, Switzerland. They drove us down to their home for our stay there. We applied for our visa to Poland and for our transit visa for East Germany. It took about a week to come. In the meantime, we preached in a number of Churches, and I spoke in a number of women's meetings. We kept busy while we were waiting.

Our visas arrived, and our plans were laid. We got the Toyota van, and it had a lot of things in it. Meanwhile, another pastor found out that we were "going in," and so he asked us if we would drive down to Luzerne: Of *course* we would if he would fill it completely for us. So, we filled the van to the max. We could not even see out the back window. We barely had enough space for our own personal things and some food. We knew to always take *food*, as the situation there was deplorable at that time. They would have money, and yet they would have to stand in lines for hours, only to get to the counter with no food to buy.

We were excited about the journey, for our burden was very real for the people of Poland. We wanted to help them so very badly. We were given a list of contacts on a paper, and in the van, we not only had clothing, but we had food and medicine as well, for we had some doctors we were to contact. Our stay was to take at least 6-8 days, and we would travel many miles distributing all the material that we had been given. We left Switzerland in the morning and arrived at the border of East Germany that evening. Our plan was to stay in the free land overnight, and we would go into East Germany early the next morning.

9b: Prison to Praise

If I remember right, I was *restless* that night. I am sure that I was thinking of many things, as crossing borders are not easy in Communist lands. It takes a very long time, sometimes many *hours* before they let you go. I do believe that it was one of the many "fear-tactics" they used, and they were not always official business. We arrived about 8:30 a.m. on the border of East Germany. The first thing they asked for was our passport, and we gave them those. Then they told us to move to the next window, and we did. They proceeded to ask why we were coming to transit East Germany, and we said, "We have heard of the plight of the Polish people, and we wanted to help them out." For some reason, they did not believe a *thing* that we said. We only had a *transit* visa for their country, which was a paper that permitted us to drive across the country, but we must not stop, and we would be watched at all times. Our papers were all in order, even the papers for the *van* that we were driving, but they did not believe what we told them. We will never know why they doubted us, but they did. That was the turning point of the whole journey for us. God knew that it would happen, and he knew that it would be part of our education in him.

We were ordered to pull the van forward and to the left side, where there was an x-ray machine waiting. The other lady and I were ordered to unload the van, while Dean was ordered to dismantle the doors and everything else that would come apart. I believe even the *dash* was involved as well. He was even ordered to tear up the floor, for materials were often hidden under the floorboards of vehicles. We learned, later, that we did not have to comply with either order.

Meanwhile, the other lady and I were unloading the van. Remember, it was so full that there was no room to even *see* out of the back windows: There were 30 large black garbage bags full of clothing plus 25 boxes of suitcases, food, medicine, etc. It was the "etcetera" that we did not know about that caused our arrest.

Every bag, box, and every container was placed through an x-ray machine to see if there was any kind of contraband involved. They would place each

255

bag, box, etc. under the scanner and announce "Yes" or "No" to indicate if it passed or failed the inspection. All the bags made it through okay, but when they scanned the boxes, we had a problem: One box failed the scanning-inspection, and immediately, the German guard said, "No! It does not pass!" Then, another group of bags passed, and another box was set aside for not passing the inspection. We did not know what they saw, but we soon were to find out. Before long, all the packages, bags, boxes, and containers had been inspected, and there sat the two mysterious boxes off to one side.

The guard turned to me and said, "Open the box!" I had nothing to open it with. So I turned to Dean and said, "Give me your jackknife." He handed me his knife, and I opened the box. Inside, there were 61 tapes on the Bible: There was no *question* that those were not allowed in their country.

The guard turned to me again, and he said, "Open the other box!" I complied, and inside the box, there was an old-fashioned mimeograph machine, with all that were needed to print material. On top of the machine was a whole group of newspaper articles concerning the solidarity movement in Poland and Lech Walsea. Immediately, we were told that we were political prisoners, and we were coming into the country to overthrow the government. Of course, none of this was true, and it had nothing to do with East Germany. Nevertheless, we had broken their laws, and we were arrested.

We were, then, told to load the van back up except for the boxes of contraband. We did what we were told, and Dean was told to re-assemble the van. I don't remember being full of fear at any time, and for that, I praise the Lord. He kept Dean and me in such peace. I am not sure as to how the other lady felt, but she was not panicking at all. I only know that we did not know about those things in the van, but if we had, we would have taken them anyway: We were called to make this trip just this way, as it was part of our destiny.

It was not as easy to get everything back in the van as it was getting everything out, and we had quite a struggle, but eventually we made it. Then, they told us to drive the van to a certain place, park it, and wait. We pulled the van into a parking place, opened the doors, and waited for the authorities to tell us the next step. It was a beautiful fall day, and it was now about 2:00 p.m. I said, "I am hungry," and I began to rummage through the good cheeses, breads, and juices that we had carried with us into these very lean countries. We all began to have some lunch, and as I sat on the edge of the van door, eating my bread and cheese, I heard God say, "Thou preparest a table before me in the presence of mine enemies, thou anointest my head with oil, my cup runneth over." (Psalm 23:5) What a great comfort his word was to my heart, and so I shared with Dean and the other lady what I heard, and they were blessed also.

As we waited, we all suddenly felt like praising, singing, and rejoicing. The Lord's Spirit was all over us, and joy bells were ringing in our hearts. We could hardly contain ourselves, for the joy of the Lord was so present. The other lady said excitedly, "If they don't do something *soon*, I will break out in praise, singing or *something*." We said that we felt exactly the same way. It was totally *opposite* of what one would normally feel in the natural. This was not natural, though; it was *God* all the way.

Our wait was very long, and it was a *fear-tactic*, which they are very good at. We could see them pull back a curtain and peek out at us to see if we were in a panic yet, and we were not. When I realized that we might be taken somewhere and *questioned*, I ate the list of contacts and delivery locations. I knew that, if the paper was found, those people would get into trouble and possibly suffer great persecution. That would never be what we wanted to bring to those wonderful brothers and sisters in the Lord.

It got to be about 4:00 p.m. when someone came and asked for the key to the van; we surrendered the key. At the time, we did not know that we had the right to refuse the request. Anyway, at about 5:00 p.m., a huge German woman guard came out to us. She stepped up to me, and through gestures and the German language, she ordered me to follow her, which I did. Dean tried to come with me, and the guard turned to him and said very loudly, "Nein!" ("No!") I said to him, "Don't worry; I will be all right." I don't know why I said it; I just knew that it was the right thing to say at the time, because he was *concerned* for me. Dean said, "Okay."

I followed the guard to a small wooden building, and inside it was an empty room. She pointed to a straight-backed chair, and I sat down. There were two people in the room with *guns* pointed at me. I found out later that Dean and the other lady were taken, sometime after me, to a *similar* room with guards and guns as well. Dean's experience was sitting over a trap door in the floor, where he thought that they might just trigger it and he would descend somewhere unknown. The other lady had a similar experience as mine. During the hour-long wait, Dean had a lot of *Scriptures* rolling around in his mind. God's word says that his word will talk with us; and it does. I found his word to be real in me as well, but most of all, I felt like I was in such peace inside. I felt like I was *looking* on this whole thing, and yet, I was actually *living* through it. I know that it seems hard to understand.

9c: Interrogation Headquarters…God's Promise…

After waiting about an hour, we were loaded into separate cars and taken to Gera, East Germany. The Interrogation Headquarters were located there at that time. It was at least an hour's drive to this location. There were three guards in the car with me, and they all had their guns trained on me. I felt very strange in such a position. As we traveled, I looked out the window, and there was the most perfect rainbow that I had seen in a long time. It was a complete bow from earth to earth. Now, the land in East Germany was very dry that year, almost a drought-effect all around. There had been no rain, and I knew that it was God's sign to us. God, then, spoke to me and said, "All the promises I have made to you, I will bring them to pass." Later, I found out that Dean had heard the same thing, and he had seen the same rainbow. God has said in his word: though the vision tarry, wait for it, it will surely come to pass. (Habakkuk 2:3) We must hang on to the promise that he has given us.

We arrived at the Interrogation Headquarters in Gera at about 6:30 p.m. They tried to make us believe that we were all alone. It was a large old house of some kind, and it was very dark and very high. I believe that there were 3 floors or more in the building. When I was getting out of the car, I saw the other cars pull up with Dean in one and the other lady in another.

We ascended the stairs one prisoner at a time, for they wanted each of us to believe that we were completely alone. They took me to a room that was typical of what one sees in movies: There was a long table with a big light overhead and a large tape recorder nearby. There was, also, a straight-back chair that I was told to sit in. They spoke to me in German, and I said, "American, I speak English." I was told to sit and wait, for they had to send for 3 people that could speak English so they could question us. Finally, a little young German man arrived, and the questioning began: Why did you come; why do you care about the Polish people; why did you bring things into our country that are against our laws; who sent you; where are you staying; who are you staying with; where did you get all these things? On, and on, and on, over, and over all night long they questioned me. They began at 7:00 p.m., and they did not stop until 7:00 a.m. They did the same with Dean and the other lady, and each of us could hear the others' voices from time to time. It was a very long night, and at one point, I became very tired. I said, "I will sleep now," and I put my head down on the desk and fell asleep for a few minutes. When I awoke, I looked up to find them all looking at me. The recorder was still running, and I said, "What did you think? I would talk in my sleep?" I believe that it was *exactly* what they thought.

They refused to believe that we did not know about the unlawful items that were in the van; but it was the *truth*, and we were all saying the same thing in 3 different rooms. At one point, they came in and tried to tell me that Dean had said something *opposite*, and I said, "No, he didn't say that." They, then, said, "How do you know he didn't say that?" I said, "Because I know my husband, and he would not say that." They looked at me very strangely and said, "Love must be a wonderful thing." I said, "It is."

Dean went through the same thing as I did, and he finally just refused to answer them. He told them that he was refusing to answer, and one of the men doubled up his fist and came to Dean as if to strike him. As he pushed his hand toward Dean, the Holy Spirit stopped him, so Dean never got hurt, thanks to God's help. Dean, then, said that he was taking the Fifth Amendment. They knew nothing of the Fifth Amendment, and they asked for an explanation. Dean said, "It is in our constitution that we can refuse to answer on the grounds that it might incriminate us." They didn't understand that at all, and they still felt that we had a plan to bring those items in, but we were all telling the same story.

The other lady was asked what she was, and she said *Pentecostal*. They, then, asked, "What is that," and for the next hour, she shared out of the *"Book of Acts"* all about the Holy Spirit. We all had opportunity to share our faith.

I really loved my interpreter. He was young, had two children, and really had been brainwashed into believing that East Germany had all that he would ever need. He told me that they had taken his children at the age of 3 and began to educate them into Communism. He said that he could ride the bus, train, etc. for 5 cents, so why would he ever want to live anywhere else. I tried to share with him how beautiful Switzerland, Austria, and West Germany were to see, but he was convinced that he had it all right there. He had nothing to compare it to, and he was taught that he had *everything*; and he *believed* it.

After they stopped interrogating me, I could sit no longer. They said that I could not get up, but I did, and I walked to the window and looked out at the people who were passing on the street. They were busy doing their daily shopping tasks, going to jobs, and all the usual things people do. My heart was so moved for them. Across the street, on a huge billboard, was a picture and a lot of writing about how wonderful the Communist government was. I said to God, "Are there any people here that love you?" He said, "There are *many* people in this city that have never bowed their knee to Communism." I prayed for all the people, but for *God's* people, I prayed that they would be strong. For the others, I prayed that they would find the Lord.

9d: Extras in the Lunch Plate

It got to be lunchtime, and they began to bring us all a plate of food. My interpreter received one too, and he ate very heartily. It was potatoes, sauerkraut, and a huge sausage that looked and smelled terrible. I know that the Germans can really make good kraut, and the potatoes were good also, but I could not stand the sausage, so I did not eat it. As I was eating the kraut, I saw something in it, and as I picked around, I saw that it was half a cockroach. I lost my appetite immediately, and I asked my little interpreter if he would like my food. He very gladly devoured it, with all the extras in it. To him, it was wonderful, but I had different idea.

It was afternoon now, and I was restless. I wanted to sing and praise the Lord, and so I began to whistle. First, I whistled *"God Bless America"; then* I whistled *"America the Beautiful."* The others heard me, and they said later that they were encouraged by it. The last song that I whistled was *"God is Able to Deliver me,"* and we felt like prisoners do when they tap out messages, so we sang and whistled ours. I really felt, "What an *honor* it is to be free to worship. It is a wonderful thing for us here in America, and how I desire it for all people."

About 4:00 or 5:00 p.m., they came and said, "Dump out all your money, as you are being fined." By this time, we were allowed to come together. Dean had given all he had, and together we had 1800 American dollars, which most would have been given to the Polish people when we went in. They said that it was not enough, and we both had to sign all kinds of papers. We signed about the fine owed; the van had to be signed over; and the food, medicine, and clothes were signed over to them as well. We had 14 days to pay the rest of the fine, which we were told was another $1400.00. That would not happen, for they had taken all the money that we had. Dean made a request for our own personal suitcases, and when we went to the van to get them, the van had been totally ransacked, and all the best things were already gone out of it. I am sure that those guards took what they wanted first.

We had about an hour's trip to the border, and we did not know what they were going to do with us at this point. We could have been left to walk out or whatever they wished. They said, "We are going to take you to a nice place for the night, and you can have whatever you want to eat. Would you like a nice steak?" We already had smelled their sausage, and we had no appetite for any more of their meat: We said "No."

They put us in a van and took us to a place called Probestella. It was a train depot and a prison, and they said that we would have a nice room. But Dean's room would not be so nice. He would have a *cot* to sleep on while we were to have beds. When we arrived in Probestella, it was not a nice place; it was a *prison*, no matter *how* you looked at it. I turned to the others and said, "It sure is not the Holiday Inn." There were *bars* on the windows and on the many places that we went through for security protections.

Dean was taken to a cell in the basement, and a small *cot* was his bed. They watched him the entire night through a window-opening in the door. He did not sleep all night, but he had a good prayer time, and he kept hearing Psalm 1, "Blessed is the man that walketh not in the counsel of the unGodly, nor standeth in the way of sinners, nor sitteth in the seat of the scornful. But his delight is in the law of the Lord, and in his law doth he meditate day and night."

It was Dean's strength for that night. It is truly wonderful how God's word is so real in times of great trial. It is alive, and it is our power in those times when all around us, it looks so dark.

The other lady and I were placed in a little better room. There were two twin beds and a small bathroom on the end. I remember trying to wash up with no washcloth, and I don't recall there being any soap. My teeth felt terrible, and they certainly could have used a good brushing. I did my best at cleansing myself, and then l lay on the bed fully clothed. Needless to say, I had no sleep, but I felt very *peaceful* in my heart. I felt the Lord very close to me, and I had a very pleasant time in prayer and meditation.

9e: The Good Samaritan

As I was lying there, thinking on the things of spirit, I heard God say, "Don't be afraid, I have a

Good Samaritan along the way for you." Now, if you know the word, you would know the story of the Good Samaritan. In the Scripture, it tells about a man that had been robbed, beaten, and left to die. Everyone that you thought would have helped him didn't; and then, a man came along who, in the natural, would have been the wounded man's *enemy*. He took him to an inn, had him fed, housed, and cared for until he was well. With this knowledge in my heart, I knew that God was telling us that, somewhere along the way, we would be taken care of. I felt his assurance in my heart that what I heard was him; and it was true, for it proved out very soon.

About 2:00 a.m., they came to get us up, and there was no dressing to do, for we had stayed in our clothing all night. They took the 3 of us to a train station where I remember having a hot drink with a guard that watched us every minute. The guard told us that we would be put on the train that was to arrive soon. We said, "We have no tickets and no money. How can we ride a train?" The man said, "That is *your* problem." I said, "No, it is not our problem, it is *God's* problem. He put us here, and he will take us out." At 3:00 a.m., they put us on the train, gave us our passports, and really just washed their hands of us.

Now, you must get the picture here: We were *exhausted*, having been awake for 24 hours; and we were *interrogated* for *12* of those hours. We did not have a *clue* as to where we were geographically, and we were all *broke*. God's presence was very real, and we knew what he had said about the Good Samaritan. We were, now, on a train with no tickets and no money. We had not washed, brushed our teeth, or changed our clothes, and Dean had not shaved and was beginning to look a little *rough* around the edges.

There we sat on the train, waiting for the conductor to come to get our tickets or our money. By now, I was not thinking clearly at all, but the Christ in me was wide-awake, and it was true of the others as well. Finally, the conductor showed up, and as usual, he asked for our tickets or our money. We had the wad of papers that we had signed behind the Iron Curtain to prove what they had done to us. And when the man asked for our fare, we said, "We have no money or tickets, for we had been literally stripped of *everything*." The little conductor could speak some English, and he said, "Just a minute." He, then, left and returned with his boss. The boss, in perfect German, told us off royally, and there was no mistaking his words, even though we understood nothing. The boss had no mercy, but the conductor did. He said to us, "I cannot let you ride the train without paying a fare." Dean said, "If you would just take us to a town, we could borrow some money on a Visa Card and pay the train company back." The conductor said, "We do not work that way." Nevertheless, he had a plan. He explained that the next stop was Bamberg, West Germany, where the United States had an army base, and he said, "They are your people; they will take care of you." We agreed to his plan; and so, he was our Good Samaritan.

We were let off at the next stop, and what surprise awaited us. There were 6 MP's waiting for us with their guns and clubs. They thought that we were some GI's who had gone AWOL or had gone over the border and had gotten drunk. They did not know what to think when 3 middle-aged Americans fell off the train. We certainly made their day, and they were a great sight to us.

They took us to the army base, fed us breakfast, and took us on a tour of the place. We were interviewed for the base's newspaper. We told our entire story to them, and they were deeply touched by it. There was a captain on the base who was married to a German woman, and he took a liking to us. We were placed in his office to wait for the banks to open so we might use our Visa Card to return to Switzerland and our friends. When the banks opened, we were taken all over seeking a bank that would accept the Visa Card, and no one in that town would take it.

Now, here we were with our people, but still no money to even get to a bank that would honor the Visa Card. Someone on the base did call around and found that, in Nuremburg, which was about 40 miles away, the bank there would take it. We still had a problem though, for we had no transportation to get there. So, we sat, and sat, and sat in the captain's office: He was *puzzled* over what he was going to do for us.

It came time for lunch, and he was going home to eat, so he decided to take us with him. He had asked us many questions about America, presidential questions, ball team questions, and just many things that he was out-of-touch with being in Germany. When we arrived at his home, we received a very cold welcome: His wife was German, and she was not sympathetic with our mission. She served us sandwiches and tea, and she really had a hard time with us there. Finally, she boiled over, and she just hollered at us, "You stupid Americans, you are always trying to save someone or get into something you have no business getting into. Now *you* have to be saved yourselves." She kept on and on, and the captain finally took her by the arm, led her into the kitchen, and closed the door; and we could hear every word. He told her, in no uncertain terms, that she was to treat us with respect, for we were his people, and she had no right to abuse us verbally. She became quiet after that. The captain let Dean use his shaver, and so Dean, at least, removed his 2-day beard, which made him feel much better.

9f: The Captain's Mercy

We returned to the base, and again, sat in the captain's office. We still had no money and could not move. Finally, later in the afternoon, the captain had a burden for us. He said, "I am going to break all the rules: I am giving you a car and a driver, and he will take you to Nuremburg to the bank. Then, you can get the money that you need to carry you back to Switzerland." He kept his word. He gave us a little black driver and an MP car with a blue light on top, and off we went to Nuremburg.

Nuremburg is a city-within-a-city: The *old* city is walled, and the *new* city encircles it. We needed to get to the bank that was in the old (inner) city, and every time the little driver would try to drive through the gate, we would end up being in the wrong lane, etc. Again and again we tried, only to be frustrated once more. The day was getting on, and the bank would be closing. Dean finally told the little driver to stop and ask a taxicab driver for help; and when we stopped, the taxicab driver turned out to be a *lady*. She said that it would be easier to *lead* us than to *tell* us, and she led us to the *exact* bank where we needed to go. We got in about 20 minutes before it closed, and Dean borrowed $500.00 so we would have enough for our stay in Europe.

Then, we asked the driver to drop us off at the train station so we could purchase our tickets for the next day to return to Switzerland. We had another confusing time finding where we wanted to go, but we managed to find it. The little driver was so patient and kind. We could not thank him enough for all that he did for us. We later sent them all a huge thank-you note, for they were truly our Good Samaritans.

After we had purchased our tickets, the other lady felt quite ill. We still had to find a place to stay for the night and get some food into us. So, when we saw a beautiful park, we told her to stay there and watch the suitcases. We would walk to find a room and then return to pick her up and go for some food. She agreed to it, and so Dean and I went to find lodging. We had no trouble finding a place, and we returned to pick up our friend.

9g: McDonald's Golden Arches

We all carried our suitcases to our room and then took time to pray for our friend; and she began to feel better. We washed up a little and went out to see where we might find food. We walked about a block or so, and when we looked up, there were the golden arches of McDonalds! Now, we don't go there very often when we are home, but it looked *so* wonderful to us that night. We had hamburgers, French fries, and Coke; and we praised God for it all! We returned to our room, showered, and fell exhausted into bed.

We slept, *really* slept, every one of us for the first time in days. How refreshing it was to all of us. We awoke early and went to the train station. We took the train to Switzerland and back to our friends. When we arrived in Winterthur, Switzerland, we took a taxi to the house where we were staying. We rang the bell, and when Bella opened the door, she took one look at us and said, "You lost it all!" I fell into her arms and cried like a baby. I had been so strong, so brave, and so peaceful; and now, here I was, a sobbing heap. Oh how *awful* I felt, so disappointed for the little Church that had given so much to us to help us on our journey. What a great *letdown* it would be when they find out that we had been stopped and everything had been confiscated, including the van.

Our little hostess Bella said, "Everyone knows what chance they take when they send illegal things in the load over Communist borders." That did not take away the pain that we felt about the loss, but she did speak the truth. She was very comforting and understanding to us.

9h: Why, Lord?

We were totally drained physically after our ordeal. Then, the presence of God, that was so heavily upon us, lifted. During the next entire week, I really had a hard time with depression. I was continually asking the Lord, "Why? Why did it happen? What are we to learn from it? Why do we still have the burden for the Polish people if we couldn't get across the borders with the good things that we had for them? Why? Why? Why?" I had to know, and I did a lot of weeping during the entire week, seeking God for answers. We visited the embassy to try to get the van back, but we had signed it over to the East Germans. We had broken their laws, so there was nothing that we could do to get it returned.

One day, I was lying across our bed, feeling so *down*. I was still asking "Why" when Dean came into the room and said that everyone was going on a hotdog roast, and he asked if I wanted to come along. I said, "No, I can't roast hotdogs until I hear from God. I will stay here alone, and maybe I will receive an answer." The family left with Dean and the other lady, and I stayed in the home alone.

I was lying there unloading my heart to the Lord: The lost goods were going to the wrong place, and we had failed him and the Polish people. All of a sudden, he spoke; it was loud and clear, and it was *wonderful*. He said, "You did not fail! The articles went right where I wanted them to go. The East Germans are my people too, and I love them as much as I love the Polish people or anyone else. You did not fail!" I shouted "Hallelujah," rose up off the bed and proceeded to praise the Lord all over the house. What a tremendous relief that swept over me. Our God is so great!

When everyone returned from the hotdog roast, I told them what I had heard, and we all rejoiced. What a tremendous relief it was for us to know that God had *planned* the entire experience of the journey, even the East Germans getting everything.

We still had a burden for Poland, and we wondered how it would be fulfilled, for we were running out of time. I was asked to speak at a woman's group; and when I did, I shared our experience, and they took up an offering. I had spoken at *many* women's meetings before this, and they *never* had taken up an offering.

That Sunday, we attended the Church that our friends went to, and the pastor came up to us and said, "Why didn't you tell us about your financial need? We would have helped you." Dean and I said, "We never beg. It is not what our God wants us to do." We thanked him for his kindness, and he handed us 100 American dollars. The offering from the women's group totaled $90.00, and we were asked to share our testimony at our friend's Church on the following Wednesday night, and they would give us an offering.

9i: The New Challenge

After the service, a man came up to me and said, "Will you go back in?" I said, "We need a vehicle and more money; if we had them, we would." He said, "I have a car, and I will get it ready for you." I said, "But we have to have the *money* as well." He said, "I will get the car ready; the money will come." He was a new Christian, and he had not yet received the baptism of the Spirit, but he was already hearing from God: He not only *heard*, but he *obeyed*. It was a real test of his faith, for we had a bad reputation now after losing one vehicle at the border.

This man went ahead and put new brakes on the car, washed it, put a blanket in it, and supplied it with Swiss chocolate, maps, and extra gas in cans in the trunk. He also made sure that we had extra coupons to purchase gas. Over there, gas was hard to find and very expensive or rationed, and so he thought of *everything*. The offering in the Church was 500 Swiss francs, which was equal to 250 American dollars at the time.

The following Friday night, the baker in the town came to visit our hostess. He was known, for miles around, as the best baker in the area. He came in with two bags of baked goods: One was all kinds of breads, and the other was all the sweet things that we all love. He came in and sat down, and our hostess interpreted for us, "He said he had been very impressed with our testimony, for we did not hate the German people, even though they robbed you."

We said, "No, we don't hate them; they were just doing their job." He was an East German man that had escaped and had come to Switzerland 20 years earlier. Therefore, he understood the oppression that the East Germans were under. He was very impressed, and God had sent him to us. Before leaving, he gave us 1000 francs, or, 500 American dollars.

We had gone "over the top" with finance, and we had the car, which was a white Mercedes -- what a car! We were going "back in"! We had not begged for one dime, and God was so very gracious to, again, bring in the money for another trip. We did not have a lot of time left, so this trip would be much shorter than our previous one.

9j: The Plan Is Given

We went to bed, and I had a dream. In the dream, I was shown the plan for the "back in" trip. I saw that we would cross into Czechoslovakia and transit the country into Poland. We could not return through East Germany, for we owed a fine there, and our information would be on the border just waiting for us. We would go to one place and *do* what we could, *leave* what we could, and return to Switzerland. God gave us the same name and address from the *previous* list that I had eaten at the East German border. We would travel to Vienna, Austria and sleep overnight; and in the morning, we would go to the embassy and get a transit visa for Czechoslovakia. After getting the visa, we would start for Poland.

We started out on a Sunday morning and traveled to Vienna. We slept in Vienna, which was a very large, busy city. We had no idea where the embassy was located. Nevertheless, in the morning, we managed to drive to the embassy as if we had done it a thousand times. We applied for and received our visa in 45 minutes, which was a *miracle*: It often takes many *hours* to get a visa. We had arrived 5 minutes before the embassy opened, and that helped too.

We were on our way again. This time, it was just Dean and I, for the other lady did not accompany us. When we came down to the wire, she said, "I am not being called for this trip." I don't know if she was fighting fear issues or if it were the facts. That is between her and her God.

We had our visa; we had our plan from God; and we had our car filled with personal items and some extras to leave behind. We were excited, and yet we had fear as well.

When we had gone to the East German border, they had stamped our passports indicating that we had *entered* the country, but they never stamped them indicating that we had *exited* the country. It was a suspicious thing, and now we were heading for *another* Communist country. I will never forget that moment in time: My heart was about to beat right out of my chest when we approached the Polish border. We had crossed the Czech border very quickly, only 40 minutes. It usually takes many *hours* to cross.

9k: Blind Their Eyes, Lord

Now would be the test. Would they see the missing stamp? Would we be questioned again? The fear rose up in me, and I began to apologize to God for being so frightened. He is so loving and understanding of our humanness. He knew that Dean and I were afraid, for there is nothing hidden from him. Remember though, he had spoken to us that courage is not the *lack* of fear; courage is *overcoming* fear and doing it anyway.

Dean had bought himself a little brown derby hat in Switzerland, and here we were in that big white Mercedes. We looked like the typical American tourists just wanting to spend lots of money in their country, and they surely *wanted* that.

We came to the border of Poland, and I was praying, "Lord, blind their eyes to the bad stamp in our passports. Don't let them ask too many questions about those things." Oh, you can imagine how I was praying, "Lord, please, please, help us." Well, he did. They asked us to give up our passports. Then, they opened the trunk and looked over the luggage, and in just a few minutes, we were Okayed to go. We had to change a certain amount of dollars into *Zlotys*, which was the Polish dollar. We would have to spend it all in Poland, for we could not bring any out. They were assured that we would help their economy, and they saw to that.

By this time of the day, it was getting into evening. We came into the town of Cieszyn, Poland. I will never forget the sense of hopelessness that I saw in the faces of the people. There was a large group of young men in the parking lot of the hotel when we arrived. They were just standing around, most of them with vodka bottles in their hands. They were either *partly* drunk or *all the way* drunk. They were loud and offensive, and I have to admit that we both were very uncomfortable getting out of the car to enter the building. We had come to the hotel because it was too dark to look for our friends. We would spend the night in the hotel, and in the morning, we would go looking for the address that we both knew was our destiny.

91: God's Great Protection

We pulled out our suitcases and entered the hotel. We were not dressed in any high fashion for sure, but we were looked over thoroughly by the desk clerk and the other workers. They took our passports and saw that we were Americans, and they charged us accordingly. The fee for us was 3,000 zlotys, which would have been an exorbitant amount for the people there: They would have been charged 20-30 zlotys. We went to our room and locked the door very well, and we began to make ourselves as comfortable as we could. Dean went into the bathroom, and I began to unpack our fresh clothes for the next day and get out some food items that we had brought with us.

All of a sudden, there was a loud knock on our door, and a voice in Polish spoke to us; and of course, we could not understand them. I didn't know what to do, as Dean was in the bathroom. So I waited a minute and asked them what they wanted, and they replied something else in Polish. I, then, went to the door; and leaving the security chain on but opening the lock, I peered out to see who was knocking. It was a woman, and she had some kind of *pills* in her hand. She said, "Sleep good, sleep good." With this, she made a motion as if laying her head on her hand. I took one look, and I immediately knew that they were *drugs* of some kind that would probably knock us out so bad that we would not awaken even if they robbed us blind. God showed me that it was the motive. I said, "No, no, we don't want them." With that, I shut the door and locked it tightly. She continued to call through the door, and I kept saying "No." Dean came out of the bathroom and asked me what had happened. I said, "Someone wanted us to sleep very deeply so they could steal our things from us." We just praised God for his care again and again.

9m: God's Warning

I could not rest at all for a long time. I had a big knot in my stomach, and I knew that I was being warned about something. Dean fell asleep, and I was glad for that. We had both been under a real strain all day, but I kept sitting on the edge of the bed, reading my Bible, praying, and waiting. All of a sudden, someone just pounded on our door very loudly; and again, some Polish words were spoken, and as before, I could not understand. They continued to pound and pound, and I suddenly yelled, "Go away, we are sleeping." They were very persistent, and about this time, *Dean* awoke. He sat up in bed and said, "What is going on?" I said, "Someone is trying to break in." The person didn't just *knock*, but they also *rattled* the door and tried to get in. Dean got out of bed, went to the door, and without opening it, he yelled as loudly as he could,

"Go away, we are trying to sleep!" Immediately, we heard a man murmur something as he went away. We believe that he thought I was alone in the room, and when he heard Dean's voice, he realized that I had a *man* with me.

Anyway, we were safe again, but for a long time, we continued to hear the man going down the hall shaking the doors, pounding, and hollering. Finally, it got quiet.

I slept a little after that, but not much, for I never felt safe there. The next morning, we ate a little and readied ourselves to find the address that God had told us to go to. We got our passports back from the hotel and began our search. I remember leaving the parking lot of the hotel and parking on the street, and we walked until we reached the address.

9n: We Find Our New Friends

We came to the house and knocked on the door. The door was opened, and we explained to the lady of the house why we had come. She was so happy, and she immediately asked where we were staying. We explained that we had stayed in the hotel the night before, but it wasn't very safe or comfortable. If she could tell us of another hotel that was better, we would like to know. She said, "You will come here, and you will stay with us. We would love to have you for as long as you can be with us." When the husband arrived, he said that, when westerners come, they always stay with them. We brought our things in and breathed a sigh of relief that we would not have to stay in that hotel again.

There were two children in the family, a boy and a girl. They were quiet, well-behaved children. We had such good talks with these people, and we enjoyed such a wonderful time of sharing together about the goodness of God. We went to encourage them, but they ended up encouraging *us*.

While we were there, we met two other couples from Poland: One was from Gdansk, which is in northern Poland, and the other couple was from the middle of Poland. They said that the believers were *strong* in Poland: They were not meeting in secret as they were in many of the *other* Communist lands; they were openly declaring their faith. The meetings that were held in Churches were often visited by the KGB, but they were not being bothered.

The man, that we stayed with, told us that the best thing that ever happened in Poland was the "Solidarity movement" through Lach Walsea. Because of all the power being shown in that movement, the KGB was very busy watching them, and they didn't have enough men to watch the believers as well. It was a *blessing* to the believers.

9o: We Visit Auschwitz

We met a number of people while we were in Cieszyn, Poland. We stayed with this couple on a Tuesday night, Wednesday night, and Thursday night. On Tuesday, the husband said, "You must visit Auschwitz while you are here." It was only a few kilometers away, and we have always had a heart for those that suffered such atrocities during that period; and so we said that we would like to do that. We were shown the way by the husband's mother. She had lost a number of her people there, so some of the areas were very hard on her. Nevertheless, she wanted to take us.

It was a deeply touching experience. We had seen it in many movies, but it was another thing to walk in those barracks and see the suitcases with names on them that had lost their lives there. We saw piles and piles of eyeglasses, and the same of human hair that had been shorn from their heads. There was every kind of cane, crutch, etc. in large piles as well. There were many clothes remaining there from those dear people. Even as I write about it, I can sense the presence of their spirits that I felt in that place. We stood in a courtyard where many had been shot just because they were Jews. What a terrible thing prejudice is, *any* kind of prejudice.

We stood in the courtyard and imagined the horrible things that had happened there. Then, a lady came up to Dean and said, "Please remove your hat; many have been killed in this very courtyard." Dean apologized immediately to the lady. We were so deeply stirred in that place, for we could sense the presence of those who had been so cruelly murdered there.

We walked through the barracks and imagined how crowded and how uncomfortable they must have been. We also imagined how cold and how *hopeless* they must have felt. A little further on were the infamous "showers" where many were gassed to death. We walked further, and there were the "ovens" that had cremated so many. At that particular spot, our friend asked to be excused: She could not go there, as so many of her relatives had perished there. We understood completely.

The camp is now a museum for all to see that what happened was real. Many refuse to believe that such things really happened, but I can tell you that they *did* happen. I have *always* believed that they happened. The victims were real people: They were real children and real parents who suffered horrible deaths. Thank God for those that survived, and as the word of God says, "They multiplied again." That was God's promise. I am so glad that we went to have this experience. It was a terrible time in human history. Let us not repeat it.

On the way back to our friends, we were stopped by the Polish police. They looked over our passports; and thank God the lady was with us. She could speak to them in Polish, and so we were allowed to go on. They had asked her many questions, and we could feel the tension in her as she answered. We thank God for her cool head: I believe that, if she had not been with us, it might have been far more difficult for us. Once again, God had gone before us and had prepared the way and our protection.

9p: Preaching in Poland

We returned to the home of our friends and their open arms of welcome. They asked us about our tour of Auschwitz, and we shared our thoughts and feelings that we had experienced in that place. They, then, asked us to preach in their Church; and we, of course, said "Yes." We were told that the KGB might come in, but just continue to minister, for they need to hear the word as well.

We went to the Church, and Dean preached that night. Interestingly, they taped his message on *Secret Service* tapes. That happened because, just before our arrival in Poland, the Secret Service had entered our friend's house and had taken away 500 blank tapes. Our friend got to thinking about that, and it came to him that it was not against the law to own blank tapes; it was against the law to have illegal *material* on them. So he went back to the Secret Service men and politely asked them to return the tapes. They could not find them, so they gave him 500 of *theirs*; and it just so happened that *their* tapes were of much better quality than *his* were.

That is just like our God: He is always blessing us in mysterious ways.

We met a lot of beautiful people in the Church that evening. So many were needing so much in the material things of life. One of the ladies was quite large in size, and she needed clothes badly. When Dean and I went to leave that location and return to Switzerland, we both went back with far less clothing than when we came. My mother had made me a number of jumpers and dresses that had a lot of ease in them, and I knew that they just might *fit* this lady. We left them (jumpers and dresses) behind, along with toiletries, chocolate, juices, money, etc. We left all that we could spare, for we needed to get home yet.

9q: God Meets the Need

Our host and hostess were receiving boxes from the West all the time. The government would go through them to make sure that they did not contain any contraband, but they were allowing a lot of things to go through. Our friends would have to *pay* to receive the package(s), so it was important that the sender shipped things that would fit the receiver or the receiver's friends. Our friend had been telling the large lady that God was able to supply her needs, and she needed a lot of things. They prayed about it, and on one of the days that we were there, a box came: It contained a large amount of clothes that fit her. God proved his love for her by that delivery, and it strengthened her faith.

Our host told Dean that, one day, he was told by God to take a bar of soap in his pocket. He didn't know why, but he obeyed. As he went out to do his errands for the day, he ran into the top Secret Service man that he had become acquainted with. The Secret Service man was bemoaning the fact of how difficult it was to obtain soap and the essentials of life. They were *rationed*, and they would receive only one bar of soap for 2 months. Our host reached into his pocket and brought out the bar of soap. The Secret Service man was so surprised, and he asked, "Where did you get this?" Our host told him how the believers "pray-in" their supplies every day. Actually, the soap had come in a package that had arrived sometime earlier. The Secret Service man was deeply touched by the small gift, and yet it was a very *large* gift to him. We take it for granted in the United States, where soap is so readily available, but it was not so in Poland during that period. It was a great opportunity for our friend to talk about the goodness and the supply of God in his life.

Our host told us another story: A lady that he knew told him how badly she needed a long-sleeve sweater, for hers was really ragged. They both prayed about it, and during our stay, a box arrived that contained a long-sleeve sweater; it was just her size. Needless to say, she was very thrilled at the goodness of the Lord.

This happened all the time to these precious people. They would pray for whatever they needed, and the items would come in: food, medicine, clothing, coats, sweaters, etc. Over and over, they watched their God come through for them. They had great faith, and it was honored.

I can remember one evening when we were to have dinner with our new friends, and the hostess had obtained a small duck to roast for the meal.

Now, anyone who has ever done much cooking knows that a duck does not have a lot of meat on it, even if it is large. There is usually just meat on the legs and back, and very little on the breast. The hostess spent time roasting the duck, and when we sat down to eat, we hardly took any, for there were 6 of us eating it. I don't remember what else we ate. I only know that it was very good, but very meager. She gave her very best, and it was very gratefully appreciated. They were so very giving with what they had.

9r: Our Time Ends in Poland

Our time with our friends was running out. We had spent the last day with them, which was Thursday; and the following morning, we would have to return to our friends in Switzerland. We had brought many little boxed drinks, Swiss chocolate, and a number of other items that would not spoil. We unloaded the car and brought the items in for them. They were so very thrilled when they saw what we had for them. The son would soon have his birthday, and the mother told us that she would keep the chocolate and the drinks for that occasion. It would make a very wonderful festive birthday for him. They were very grateful for all that we did.

It was with great sadness that we left this wonderful couple. We left all the rest of the Polish zlotys and a number of American dollars for them. The man told us that the American dollar goes a long ways in that place. He could purchase a number of items with very little American money. We took their address, so when we would return home, we would send them many packages to help them out. We also wrote down everyone's size so they would not waste their money to receive the packages. I am sure that the packages that we would send (and packages sent by others) were God's way of answering their prayers again.

We got back on the road on Friday morning and headed for our home in Switzerland. We, again, went across the borders very easily, and we arrived back at our friend's home on Saturday night. Everything went so well for us, and we were grateful. Our friends in Switzerland were very glad to see us again, and they were very happy that our car had not been seized and that we had not been detained in any way.

When we arrived, we called the little brother who had so graciously lent us his car. He was so thrilled to hear that we were back safely, and he came right away to pick up his car. He had told the Lord that he wanted to go on *vacation* when he was told by the Lord to lend us his car. He had a bit of an argument with God, but he said "Yes" in the end. We are so grateful to that man for being the hand of God in our lives to help us fulfill the burden that we had for those beautiful Polish people.

We rejoiced with our Swiss friends about the trip, and we talked for many hours and shared all we had done and seen. We told about our Auschwitz experience, and they were glad that we had the opportunity to see something while we were gone. They could tell, by our sharing, that we had been deeply moved by our going there. Most of all, we were rejoicing that our mission had been accomplished, and our burden had been lifted. Now, there were peace and release from the assignment that God had laid on our hearts, and we were ready to return to the United States.

Chapter 10: Home Again

10a: The Burden Is Lifted: We Return to the United States

We stayed another day with our friends in Switzerland, and on Monday, we flew out of Zurich Airport to return to our homeland. We had a wonderful time: Yes, even the *prison* experience was wonderful. We learned more from that experience than we ever could have learned from books. It was a life-changing experience, not just knowledge gained through some words written on paper.

I remember looking out the plane window and thinking of how far we had come in *miles*, in our *faith*, and in our *understanding* of how God loves his creation. He loves *all* of us, not just a certain group that does everything right. Yes, God *loves* us all and *lives* in us all: "That was the true light, which lighteth every man that cometh into the world." (John 1:9)

God sees so much higher than we do, and his purpose is so much greater than our little minds can fathom, unless he reveals himself to us. His love is so pure! It is so very real and powerful in our lives. How we love him more and more each day.

When we returned, we were welcomed with open arms by our parents and by our friends that we had been ministering to all across the United States and Canada. We were asked to go to many places and share our *"Prison to Praise"* experience.

Everywhere that we went, our story blessed and challenged many, many people. Many responded by sending packages to our friends. Some responded by donating money, and many were challenged to pray more for others. There was a challenge for everyone through our experience. We never know, when we say "Yes" to the will of God, how far it will carry us or what will be required of us before it is finished.

10b: More Road Work

For the next 2 years, we traveled extensively and ministered God's word. We were in-and-out of many areas, many Churches, and certainly every level of understanding of the word. We were glad to go and share what we knew, what we had seen, and what we had experienced. It was after this when a group of Spirit-filled Catholics, to whom we had been ministering, asked us to stop traveling and teach them the word of God. After much praying, we said "Yes," and for that period in our lives, the traveling stopped.

We were called to Haiti during our time of teaching these people. I felt led by God's Spirit to arrange a trip to Haiti to expose this group to another part of the world. It is a country dark with Voodoo, and it was near to travel to. We gathered 26 people to make the trip. I made all of the arrangements myself as to the hotel where we would stay, the collecting of the monies for the trip, the purchase of the tickets, etc. I did not make any itinerary of what we would do, for the Lord said that he would arrange it. I trusted him to do it. When we arrived in Haiti, we were never without a place to preach. In fact, it became necessary to form 5 or 6 groups of people to be able to do all that we were being asked to do. We would put someone that could minister the word with those that played an instrument or could sing.

They would be taken by a pastor to their Church, where they would bring the sermon, teach new songs, minister to the people one-on-one, and in general, just do whatever God showed them to do.

What a tremendous time of ministry that we all had there. God just led us each day, and with all the need that surrounded us, many had no money left when we departed the country. It was a very sad, depressing, needy country. The people that we met and ministered to were not depressed, for they knew the Lord and his goodness. There was much hunger; we saw it everywhere; and people were living in cardboard boxes everywhere. We all had our eyes opened as to the blessing of God in our lives here in the United States. We had taken many suitcases filled with school supplies to give away, and the schools were very thankful for all that we brought. We had taken a number of young people with us, and they had life-changing experiences while they were there.

10c: Time to Return Home

All of our lives were *changed* while ministering in this beautiful yet Spiritually-dark land. We had stayed in a nice hotel; we had eaten every day, some excellent meals; and the waiters were very kind to us.

Meanwhile, whenever the waiters would serve us, we did not leave them any tip, because we all had agreed to give each of them a larger, one-time tip before leaving for home. With the larger "payoff," the waiters could better meet their financial needs.

One day, one of the waiters asked me, "Have we taken good care of you each day?"

I answered, "Yes, you have."

He asked, "Then, why do you not *tip* us?"

I replied, "Because, when we are ready to leave, you will be *glad* that we didn't give you anything each day."

Then, on the last day that we were there, we called all the waiters into one of the rooms and handed each of them a brand new pair of socks. The waiters accepted the socks and looked at us as if we were crazy.

We instructed, "Look inside," and they found a brand new $50.00 bill. They were overjoyed at the thought of what all that money could do for them. One waiter said that it would pay off all his debts. They all agreed that they were happier to receive the *larger* amount of money at the *end* of our stay than they would have been if they had received the *smaller* amount each day. Our hearts were filled with joy to see how happy we had made them.

The next day, we went to the Port-au-Prince Airport to fly home.

"Home," what a wonderful word. It never mattered where we traveled: It was always a joy to land again on American soil. This land is truly our home. After so many opportunities to see so much of the world, we would always feel *at peace* whenever we would put our feet on our homeland.

In any event, by the time we arrived at the airport, many among our party had been so *moved* (by the extent of poverty of those whom we had met) that they literally had given away their last dime. We had *warned* everyone to put away enough money for the *airport tax*, because we would not be permitted to leave the country without paying it. Obviously, many of the less-experienced members had bigger hearts than wallets. Therefore, Dean and I ended up paying their share of the tax so that we all could board the plane and fly home.

Incidentally, Dean and I had *suspected* that some of the less-experienced members would fail to put away enough money to pay their airport tax, and therefore we ourselves had put away enough money for such "emergency."

Anyway, we (Dean and I) would make many more journeys in the years to come, some long distance and some short. We did a lot of teaching right here at home in Port Huron, Michigan, and we kept our ears open for God's call to other places.

Our lives have been full, rich, exciting, and exhausting; but we are and always will be eternally grateful that God *did* call us and allow us to go and do all that He had chosen for us.

We are not our own; we were bought with a price, and we must remember that. We are here to *serve*, not to make a name for ourselves or to heap up treasure. Dean and I are doing our best every day to remember this message and to do God's will.

We do pray that our story has been an inspiration to you.

God bless you.

Afterward

Please let us say that we are not against any Church, denomination, nationality, race, creed, or color. All people are created by God in his image, and he makes no mistakes. He lives in every person if they could only see that. He has a plan for everyone, and we are not here by mistake.

We (Dean and Connie) have had tremendous moves of God's Spirit in Churches and in homes. God is not confined to any space, for he fills all spaces. What we experienced was very unusual, and it was our experience and no one else's. What we learned was direct from God's Spirit through direct experience, for he never called us to attend any Bible school. We are not against those either if you are called to go. With our hands on journey, we saw a lot of bondage in religious systems. God's word says, "…where the Spirit of the Lord is, there is liberty." (2 Corinthians 3:17) That is what we did not see a lot of as we traveled in denominations. There seems to be some unwritten law that is their agenda, and God does not have much room to do what he wants sometimes. The thing that we are against in people's lives is guilt, fear, and bondage of any kind. Jesus Christ came to set us free of these things. If your life is such that you are called into some kind of Church, then stay there and do all you can with all of your might. We did for years ourselves, until God said something different to us.

Our prayer is that you find your own way, not someone else's. Follow God with all your heart, soul, mind, and strength. Therein lies your peace.

AND SO WE SAY. . . IT IS FINISHED! AMEN
AND AMEN.

Shalom